IF I'M SO
Spiritual,
WHY AM I STILL
So Anxious?

HOW TO FIND YOUR CENTER
AND RECLAIM YOUR JOY

JOY STONE

ISBN: 978-19-5-315322-7

Published by

If you are interested in publishing through Lifestyle Entrepreneurs Press,
write to: *Publishing@LifestyleEntrepreneursPress.com*

Publications or foreign rights acquisition of our catalog books.
Learn More: *www.LifestyleEntrepreneursPress.com*

Printed in the USA

This is for Eric and Jack.
Thank you for being my joyful companions
in this precious life.
You make me smile every day.

Contents

Foreword

I feel honored that Joy asked me to write the foreword to this book. This book will touch your heart deeply. You may find yourself reading it over and over again. It is possible that each time you read *If I'm So Spiritual Why Am I Still So Anxious?* you will discover new parts of yourself and more fully understand your psyche.

A true master is someone who is able to take complex ideas and make them simple and understandable for the common woman or man. Joy Stone's *If I'm So Spiritual Why Am I Still So Anxious?* offers a piece of heaven on earth for all of us to enjoy. Joy effortlessly weaves storytelling with real-life experience and knowledge from the ancient texts of yoga to form a delightful and colorful tapestry.

We call the master an *acharya* if they have walked this road before us and figured out how to manage the obstacles on that path. Joy is an *acharya* of living with anxiety. She teaches us how to see anxiety as a delivery service that has an important message for us. Our job is to listen closely to this message. For Joy, anxiety is not a problem to be overcome; it is simply a symptom telling us that something inside of us has become disconnected. We need to go to Soul School with Joy to learn how to listen and reconnect with that still small voice inside.

Joy describes what the ancient texts of yoga say about the true nature of the mind. It is fickle. This is your current reality, but your reality can change at any time. Don't get too attached to your precious thoughts because you do not have as much clarity as you think you have. When you are feeling anxious, your mind is not clear. The anxiety is asking you to take another look at your reality. This is a revolutionary concept. Many times, we attempt to numb the anxiety, push it away, or assume the anxiety is real. But what if instead you moved closer, closed your eyes, and tilted your head in an attempt to hear what your deeper self wants to tell you. Your deeper heart says, "Come home to me." It is the anxiety that is the precious call of the wild taking you inward. The courage to lean inward is a beautiful expression of self-love.

When reading *If I'm So Spiritual Why Am I Still So Anxious?* you will begin to transform your smaller perception of reality and learn how to perceive a reality that includes more data points, the history of why things have turned out the way they have, and compassion from a place beyond your small self. You will learn that a big part of being human means that we have all experienced abuse, trauma, and pain. We are here to understand that we are all connected through our suffering, and only then can we decide how and when to set appropriate boundaries to keep ourselves safe in this human experience.

This book has many practical exercises that take us from the esoteric and abstract spiritual teachings of yoga and guide us into the practical application of the ancient teachings in the context of the modern world. This book is a sincere gift in these times of fear and instability. Any of us can sit down with this book, a cup of tea, and a pad of paper and be led through an incredibly deep experience on a Sunday afternoon. The book is as useful as it is inspirational, which is a rare combination.

Amy Wheeler, PhD
President of the International Association of Yoga
Therapists (2018 to 2020)

CHAPTER 1

The Problem with Anxiety

*"If you feel lost, disappointed, hesitant, or weak,
return to yourself, to who you are, here and
now and when you get there, you will discover
yourself, like a lotus flower in full bloom, even
in a muddy pond, beautiful and strong."*

—Masaru Emoto

The problem with anxiety is that it's never been *your* problem. In fact, I bet you already know a lot about your anxiety. You can list every single one of your triggers because you've spent years in self-discovery analyzing them. You've learned to reframe your thoughts, and you've taken more deep breaths than anyone else you know. You have overcome obstacles and have come a long way in your life despite the worry, self-doubt, and fear you often live with.

In your desire to be better and feel better, you have a mountain of self-help books by your bed, and you're

5

always on the look-out for the next best one. You've attended more mind-body workshops, retreats, and yoga classes than most ever will. You've meditated, journaled, and maybe even chanted mantras.

You believe in the goodness of the universe, consider yourself spiritual, and know that you are part of something bigger than yourself. You do your best to be grateful, mindful, and happy. Yet even with all of that, you *still* struggle with negative thinking, worry, self-doubt, uncertainty, indecision, and fear. Anxiety persists.

Part of the frustration with your spiritual practice and techniques is that they were *never* designed to *fix* you. What is anxiety if it's not the problem you thought it was? And what is the meaning of your spiritual practice if not to solve your "brokenness"? How does one become happy, joyous, and free?

These are the questions I'll be helping you answer in this book. It will be through these new insights and clarity about anxiety, spirituality, and who you truly are that I believe will finally set you free. I didn't come to these conclusions easily or purely academically. I came to know them through years of personal experience and by working with hundreds of clients just like you. This is the exact dilemma I found myself in more than a decade ago. It is the same crisis so many of my clients come to me now to help them solve.

The Mud

"What are you doing here?" Emily asked with her head tilted and a smirk on her face I'll never forget. Shame filled my whole being. My heart dropped, and my stomach sank. I was thirteen years old, attending the only dance I would ever attend in all of my school years. I already knew I didn't belong there – I knew I wasn't loveable – but she made sure everyone else knew it too.

Going to that middle school dance was a conscious practice in courage. It took every ounce of bravery I could gather to show up. I desperately wanted to be part of something. I wanted to belong. I wanted to be loved and accepted. I went into the bathroom and cried. I didn't let anyone see me. I was good at being strong, just like I know you've been in your life too. The thing about anxiety is that few people from the outside can see it. It's mostly happening on the inside. It's a lonely desperation, and if you don't show it, no one will ever know. You're good at hiding it.

Every immediate caregiver in my life was an alcoholic. I'd witnessed men abuse and beat my mother, strangers beat my dad, and my four-hundred-pound grandmother get so drunk that she'd fall asleep with a whiskey and Coke in one hand and a Salem menthol in the other. I was forced to take on responsibilities no thirteen-year-old should ever be asked to.

That dance was a chance for me to be normal. It was an opportunity to be like all the other kids at school. But at that moment at that dance, I realized there would be no normal. I stuffed it down and went on, just like I always did, and just like I know you do.

About four years before that dance, I spent less than a year living in California with my dad. He decided to leave Seattle and head back to his hometown for work. Together, we convinced my mom to let me go with him. My dad was funny, handsome, creative, and loving. He was one of the best people I've ever known. But he also had a terrible drinking problem. When he was drunk, he'd turn into a completely different person. When I was about six years old, I remember telling him how much I wanted a chalkboard. He replied, "How does it feel to want?" Once, when we were living in California, he arrived at my school so intoxicated he crashed into a tree. Shortly after that, I went to stay with my aunt and uncle. They eventually called my mom and told her it was time to come get me.

My mom and her new husband, another alcoholic guy I barely knew, arrived to take me back to Seattle. My dad and I waited for them on the front porch of the cockroach-infested apartment that we lived in together before I went to stay with my aunt and uncle. My dad looked defeated and ashamed. My heart ached for him, and for me. Why didn't he love me enough to stop drinking? Why couldn't he take care of me? At nine years old, I didn't understand that alcoholism is an illness that leaves the sufferer powerless.

I was back in Seattle and about to be a big sister. My mom was pregnant. I was ten years old and certain this was going to be the start of something wonderful. The fact that I hated my mom's new husband, and that we lived in a tiny one-bedroom apartment directly attached to the local tavern was of small concern to my young brain. My mom, a bartender with a drinking problem and a habit of staying out until the bar closed, was going to have to stay home with me. There wouldn't be any more scary nights waiting up for her to come home. Six months after my brother was born, my mom and stepdad were approved for low-income government-subsidized-housing about fifteen miles north of Seattle. Our new place was in a large low-income-looking complex with two- and three-bedroom townhomes. In the middle of the development, there was a playground and a basketball court. For the first time, at age eleven, I'd be in a neighborhood with other kids and have my own bedroom. I couldn't wait to decorate it.

Things didn't turn out as I'd planned. The next seven years would be filled with the same instability, fear, and shame I'd lived with since birth. But like every other pre-teen, I was driven by a need to belong and fit in with my peers. I wanted to have fun, explore life, and discover myself. Instead, I was weighed down with the overwhelming responsibilities of an adult. My real dad was gone. My stepdad was kicked out – thank goodness –and my mom was busy living life with her friends at the bar. There was no space for me to be a young girl developing her confidence and exploring her individuality. I had to survive and figure things out, fast. I was left home alone to raise my infant brother. I had to play mother when I had never been mothered and be there for him when no one was there for me. I remember making many phone calls to the bar, begging my mom to come home. She'd always promise she was on her way home, but she usually wasn't. There were more mornings than I can count when I didn't make it to school. Either my mom hadn't made it home from the night before, or my grandmother, who lived in the same complex, wouldn't babysit my brother just to punish my mother. I remember one morning, in particular, I pleaded with my grandmother to take my brother so I could go to school. Hacking through her menthol cigarette, she told me what a loser my mom was. My anxiety mounted as I watched the clock move past the time I knew the school bus would arrive. I missed it.

Anxiety was anchored into my nervous system. It had become my default state. Any childlike nature I might have had was long gone. For me, it was all about survival. The constant stress created rashes on my body, cognitive difficulties, and a negative self-image. My mind was constantly distracted by thoughts of not being good enough and the need for stability. I became a chameleon that sought approval by doing and being whatever anyone needed. My mind and body felt disconnected. If there was a spark of light within me, I didn't know where it was.

Anxiety depletes your energy. It limits your ability to be comfortable in your own skin. It diminishes your confidence and joy. It takes effort for you to push aside your anxiety, and self-doubt, as you present your happy image to the world. You are constantly doing your best to quiet the mental noise while simultaneously wondering why the chatter is still there.

At eighteen, I left home. I was free, or so I thought. I had terrible guilt about leaving my brother behind. When he was younger, he would sometimes call me "Mommy." The situation was complicated, but I had to put on my oxygen mask first. I had to survive. I rented an apartment with a girl in the neighborhood I'd become friends with. We shared some of the same childhood histories, and she was as disappointed in life as I was. But together we were going to take control of our future and find our way in this world.

When you're desperate and anxious, you look for any way out of the darkness. I've learned that wherever there is suffering, there is a solution, but it's almost never what we think it is. Getting out of my childhood home was the absolutely necessary first step and the obvious right choice. I had removed myself from the conditions that were creating my stress, but the anxiety would persist even after I left. Before things would get better, they had to get much worse. The next six years would be an escalation of mental and emotional suffering that would lead to spiritual bankruptcy and a bottom that would ultimately change my life forever.

After I moved out, my life started looking successful by conventional standards. I had a cute apartment, new friends, a good job, and I was taking classes at the community college. People would praise me for being strong, capable, and responsible. (I became addicted to those compliments because of how other people felt about me controlled how I felt about me.)

My anxiety got worse, not better. I was free from the responsibilities and stressors of my childhood, but not from the fear of not being good enough or my uncertain future. Anxious thoughts took over my mind. In social situations, my tongue was tied, my body would sweat, and my heart would race. The terror of saying the wrong thing or being rejected would impair my ability to function properly.

Anger and jealousy began rearing their ugly heads. I didn't feel like anyone understood me. I had this bitter belief that life was easier for everyone else. I was stuck in the toxic realm of blame. I blamed my mom, my dad, my grandmother, and the string of abusive and alcoholic men that were brought into my life. I especially blamed alcohol. I would never ever drink like them.

A Turning Point

The night before May 27, 1996, was one of the many nights I drank too much. I wasn't trying to get drunk; I was just trying to have fun and enjoy life. Didn't I deserve that?

I had no intention of losing control. But for some reason, I had. I noticed I would drink my beer a little faster than everyone else, and I'd drink a little more. I wanted another one and another one. Sometimes my personality would change.

I knew better. I hated what alcohol did to my family. It destroyed my childhood. Why couldn't I control how much I drank? I was baffled. I'd assert all of my willpower, but I just couldn't control the amount of alcohol I drank once I started drinking. Sometimes my anxiety would be so intense all I could think about was getting a drink. Alcohol was the only thing that relieved my anxiety. It was the only thing that made me feel normal. I'd have a few drinks and – poof – I could suddenly say all the right things, and I felt comfortable in my skin. In my mind, I became funny, pretty, and popular. I didn't worry about the future or the shame of my past. Alcohol changed the way I felt about myself. I craved more of that feeling. The consequences became shameful, but I'd tell myself the price had to be paid. I would do anything not to feel the anxiety or the unworthiness, self-doubt, and fear.

But the next morning, when I woke up, I knew something was different. I'd just turned twenty-four, and I felt tired. The cycle had to stop. But how? All of my best thinking and best ideas had gotten me to that morning. My anxiety was at an all-time high. I knew I needed help.

But I was also capable and strong. I'd survived what so many kids hadn't. I was a miracle. I remember hearing a counselor say that kids like me usually end up dead or in prison. But not me. I was launched into this world with nothing and still managed to look normal. I created the perfect façade. It was the inside I couldn't rearrange and patch up. It was the relentless anxiety and the unworthiness, fear, and shame that I couldn't out-run. I hit bottom.

Thankfully, at that moment, I was humbled just enough to finally ask for help. That day became the last day I ever had a drink. Months later, my first mentor, an angel who introduced me to a new way of living, called it a moment of clarity. She told me that Grace – the universe, love, light, God, whatever you call it – is always present, it's just that sometimes we're not awake until we are.

I'd never heard such a thing. I was of the mindset that we were on our own. I thought we had to earn love, attention, and approval to get rid of that gaping hole inside. Yet there she was, telling me there was a beautiful way out, or rather a way into the Truth of who we are – which is confidence and joy – and that we are always loved, no matter what.

Anxiety separates you from yourself. It keeps you from experiencing your inner joy. Anxiety is a coping mechanism that doesn't work in the long term. Just as the alcoholic picks up the drink to calm their irritability, you sometimes engage in hours of worry, rumination, and negative thinking to quiet your inner fear and uncertainty. The alcoholic is asked to put down the drink but can't do it. You're told not to worry but can't stop. You both are addicted to your drug of choice. And why not? It worked for a while, didn't it?

Throughout this book, I will continue to share some of my personal story, the seven spiritual principles that enabled me to find freedom from anxiety, and transformational stories of clients I've coached who have embodied these principles and reconnected to their confidence, wisdom, and joy.

My sincere wish for you is that, as you read this book and practice these principles in your life, you can say, "I'm not anxious anymore because I am deeply connected to my inner joy and guided by my inner truth."

CHAPTER 2:

Letting Go of Labels

"Be like the lotus: trust in the light, grow through the dirt, believe in new beginnings."
—Anonymous

During the early years of my sobriety, and with the support of so many, I rebuilt my life. I found an exciting career in the travel industry and worked my way into a coveted sales position with bonuses, benefits, and a great salary. I flew all over the world, enjoying new adventures. I met the love of my life, and together we moved from Seattle to Los Angeles so he could pursue his dream in the music industry. I became part of a community and had friends. I lived with the security, love, and resources I'd always wanted. I even found a therapist who was spiritually driven, and who introduced me to ancient teachings and concepts such as "Thoughts create your reality," "What you think, you become," "Everything is energy," and "The essence of the universe is love." I read books such as *As a Man Thinketh*, *A Return to Love*, *You Can Heal Your Life*, *Psycho-Cybernetics*, and *Sermon on the Mount*, and I heard about channeled work and literature such as *The Yoga Sutra* and *A Course in Miracles*.

It was official. I was a spiritual seeker on a spiritual path doing all the things that were sure to bring me inner peace and joy, right?

The frustration was huge. I would make progress then fall back into the hole of anxiety. Only my husband and a few friends knew what went on. I hadn't had a drink in almost ten years, so I couldn't ease my anxiety with alcohol. Instead, I'd read another book, go to another meeting, schedule another session with my spiritual therapist, work harder, organize my house, or whatever I could do not to feel anxious.

One morning, out of the clear blue sky, I woke with the certainty that I was to become a yoga teacher. I'd never done yoga except for a few times at the YMCA and the local gym. I didn't enjoy it much because it was too slow for my anxious mind. I was not a yogi, but something deep inside was calling me to study yoga. I felt an inner need to immerse myself in this ancient healing art, which I knew nothing about, except for the tiny bit I had read about in the books my spiritual therapist had introduced me to.

Later that week, I made a trip over to a local yoga studio to inquire about opportunities. As I walked in, I noticed a sign promoting their new soon-to-begin teacher training. I talked to the manager and immediately expressed my desire to sign up. She asked if I practiced yoga. I wanted to lie and say "yes," but, instead I told the truth and said, "no." I assured her I was serious and that I had to be part of the training. She said it was the first-ever teacher training the studio was offering, and she'd have to talk to the owners and get back to me.

Getting accepted into that yoga teacher training was the beginning of a rebirth. It was divine intervention. I wasn't a particularly intuitive person at the time, but I knew I was being led. I cried when all of us trainees gathered in our first circle and shared our stories. I was in the right place. It was the first time in my life I wasn't being motivated by fear. I was listening to my heart.

This new journey, a profound extension of every step I had ever taken up to that point, had given me the unshakeable courage to ask myself, "Who are you?" and to finally say, "You belong here."

A New Beginning

For my students, I was driven to become the best yoga teacher I could be. I was one of less than five hundred teachers in the world to be certified in a comprehensive, holistic school of yoga that emphasized spiritual philosophy and psychology as much as it did the poses.

I followed a need to solve my inner suffering. Anxiety still loomed. I'd feel great on my yoga mat, in a meditation circle, or at a workshop, but I still shrunk inside whenever someone hinted at disapproval. I worried about the future and still struggled with fear.

By the age of thirteen, I had been emotionally, physically, and sexually abused and was homeless, neglected, and abandoned. I was asked to keep secrets I couldn't bear. I once took the Adverse Childhood Experience (ACE) questionnaire. It includes ten questions that determine your level of childhood trauma and the effects it can have on your life. It is a test where ten out of ten is not a good thing. Questions cover topics such as alcohol or drug abuse of primary caregiver; depression of a primary caregiver; childhood experiences of physical, sexual, and verbal abuse; neglect; a sense of not feeling loved; a lack of basic needs such as food, clothing, or shelter; the sight of a caregiver being abused; and divorce or separation. I scored a nine out of ten.

When I was twenty-six years old, I was diagnosed with post-traumatic-stress-disorder (PTSD). It was true I'd experienced trauma as a child, but I didn't want to be labeled by it. These words of Krishnamurti resonated deeply with me: "The day you teach the child the name of the bird, the child will never see that bird again." When you are labeled, it becomes easy to mistake the disorder for who you are. You forget about your true nature, which is whole and complete, and instead see yourself as fractured through the lens of your diagnosis. It becomes your identity.

I grew up thinking I was unworthy and needed to be fixed. I was tired of that. I searched for something else.

In spiritual books, I'd read about a deep-within kind of contentment. But somehow it eluded me. I'd tried everything from traditional treatments such as therapy and medication to alternative medicines like sound healing, acupuncture, yoga, chakra balancing, meditation, herbs, and oils. They provided me some relief, but I was still struggling with anxiety.

Through friends, I learned about a yoga teacher who'd spent years traveling back and forth to India studying with both T.K.V Desikachar, a revered yogi, and his son, Kaustaub Desikachar. He then lived in Los Angeles, teaching students what he'd learned, which centered around an ancient foundational text of yoga called *The Yoga Sutra*, the same channeled work my spiritual therapist had loosely introduced me to almost a decade earlier.

The Yoga Sutra is distinct from the poses, which are often equated with yoga here in the West. Instead, it's one of the six philosophies that emerged from the ancient Indian Vedas or scriptures. It's a complete guide for living, and one of the oldest systems of healing on the planet. *The Yoga Sutra* is designed to help people reduce suffering and create more sustained joy in their lives by transforming the mind.

The yoga teacher agreed to see me, and we met privately for weekly sessions. It was a magical time. I still remember the taste of chai tea and the smell of frankincense. I was being exposed to new ideas such as "Suffering begins at the level of the mind," "Life is happening from you, not to you," and "Pain is universal, but suffering is optional." Part of me enthusiastically embraced these concepts while the other part of me was deeply offended. On one hand it all made sense, but on the other hand it was ridiculous. I didn't choose my childhood. I didn't choose the abuse and neglect. How was my suffering optional? I was confused, but I wanted to learn more.

In one particular session, we studied Sutra 1:2, which outlines the definition of yoga from *The Yoga Sutra* as "the calming of the turbulence of the mind." A little light bulb lit up in my head. I'd been trying to manage, control, and resist my feelings of anxiety, not necessarily calm my mind. I'd heard it said that "what you resist persists and what you focus on expands." A new insight emerged. It was a subtle distinction, but it began to change the direction of my practice.

Yoga's power lies in how it can help you transform your mind. The Buddha said, "With your thoughts, you make your world." Without the skill of conscious choice and disciplined focus, your mind will unconsciously wander. A group of regions in your brain cause your mind to automatically and unconsciously assume what something means, to create judgements and opinions, and to travel to the past and the future – anything but focusing on what is actually happening right here and right now. Scientists call this your brain's default mode network (DMN). Eastern traditions like yoga call this wandering "your monkey mind." It is a network – or monkey mind –

which can *manufacture* anxiety by creating fears, worries, or outcomes that don't exist at this moment.

A New Direction

My soul nudged me in a new and unexpected direction. I read that approximately forty million American adults – roughly eighteen percent of the population – struggle with anxiety. I wanted to teach spiritual seekers, like me, who were still struggling with anxiety and self-doubt, the philosophy, psychology, and practices that were radically changing my life.

One night in bed, while reading through a magazine, I came across an article featuring a program in positive psychology – the science of happiness and optimal human flourishing – that was being led by former Harvard professor Tal-Ben Shahar. The program was starting soon. The next day, I secured my spot and was soon on my way to Stockbridge, Massachusetts.

During a lecture in the program, my teacher, said, "The things that make you less depressed aren't always the things that will make you happy." The truth of that hit me hard. I knew it applied to anxiety too. The things that make you less anxious aren't always the things that will make you happy. I experienced another spark of insight. I'd spent years of energy trying to either run away from or control my fear, but either way, my focus was mostly on the problem.

As a spiritual seeker, you sometimes find yourself at a point in your spiritual journey where you've analyzed and studied your anxiety but you're still struggling and wondering why. You've thrown every spiritual tool you can think of at your fears and doubts, and you feel better but not great. Deepak Chopra writes, "The solution is never at the level of the problem; the solution is always love, which is beyond problems."

Back in Los Angeles, I began studying with another teacher who was opening my heart and mind to new ways of experiencing *The Yoga Sutra* and my practice. She not only had her Ph.D., but she was a yoga therapist and a respected new thought leader in the field of mental health. Like me, she was blending the modern Western science of optimal human flourishing with the ancient Eastern healing wisdom of *The Yoga Sutra*. And, like my former teacher, she'd also been a student of T.K.V. Desikachar and had spent more than a decade going back and forth to India.

A Shift in Perception

Through this relationship with my new teacher, I experienced a powerful shift in my perception. *Abhyasa* is a Sanskrit word that means practice. But it is not the practice of touching your toes or standing on your head – I could do all of that, and I was still internally bound. Instead, it is the daily continuous practice of becoming on the inside what you want to experience on the outside. *Abhyasa* refers to the practice or discipline of achieving a tranquil state of mind and a state of harmony with one's self. I realized I had to make a decision. Would I continue to practice becoming less anxious, or would I commit to becoming confident and joyful? Would I commit to living in trust or fear? It's easy to mistake the tool for the answer, but the spiritual tool is there only to serve your commitment to reclaim your joy and reconnect with who you truly are.

Samadhi is a Sanskrit word that means "to be in a state of wholeness or completeness." This is a state where your mind is free from anxieties and fears. It is in this state where your intuition and joy can truly emerge. As you go through life, you can become blocked from this part of who you are. You build a protective layer to hide your fears and limiting beliefs such as "I'm not enough." Then, you create an image or façade which you present to the world. Being in a state of deep joy involves both the letting go of this façade and the embracing of a new identity, all of which requires trust and faith.

How I finally reached this experience in my life was by living and embodying the teachings and principles this book contains. I've been on this journey for almost twenty-four years. The gratitude I feel for where I am today is beyond words. I know for sure it is the inner work that will detangle you from your anxieties, fears, and self-doubt. However, as a spiritual student, a beginner's mind is essential. Otherwise, you will just continue to filter new information through your old beliefs.

I've been blessed with opportunities to study with some of the greatest thought leaders and spiritual teachers in the world. Yet, it was the application of what I learned that changed me. Spiritual life is not an academic endeavor. It is a practice of unlearning and awakening. In yoga therapy, we are taught that transformation is a process of repetition, digestion, assimilation, and elimination. You can experience profound and positive change when you open your mind, develop faith, and commit to the process.

The years between my first yoga teacher training and today have provided some of my most profound spiritual awakenings and potent personal life lessons. It was a pivotal spiritual turning point – a flash of clarity – while sitting in my car on my birthday, which I will share with you in this book, that would radically open my eyes to a new way of living.

Do I ever still experience anxious feelings or self-doubt? Yes. That's part of the human condition. But I exist on a new footing. I am established in the truth of who I am, and through consistent, committed practice, I have created a positive and empowering chosen identity and a way of relating to myself and my life. You can too.

The seven spiritual principles you'll discover in this book are part of the essential fabric of my private coaching practice and group coaching program, Soul School, from which I have helped countless men and women experience the same freedom from anxiety and inner joy that I live with today.

Your anxious mind likes familiarity and therefore wants to keep you where you are. To that end, it creates obstacles, worst-case scenarios, and stories about why you're not enough or not doing enough. But these stories aren't the truth of who you are, and they don't represent what you are capable of. What you will find in this book will help you reconnect to your inner guidance system and create a new and liberating reality from the inside out.

CHAPTER 3

The Spiritual Principles

"However powerful or disturbing something
may appear to be, it is our reaction to it that
determines its effects"

—T.K.V. Desikachar

D uring my positive psychology program, I was introduced to a powerful story, originally revealed by Dr.
Hans Selke, an internationally renowned Canadian phy-
sician and scientist known as the father of stress.

Two young brothers were raised in the same abusive
home by an alcoholic father. They, unfortunately, endured
tremendous stress, fear, and anguish. As the boys grew
older and entered adulthood, they left their childhood
home, each going their different ways in the world, taking
separate paths with differing priorities, beliefs, and life
decisions. Years later, they were interviewed separately
by a psychologist who analyzed the effects and scars of
alcoholism and divorce on children. Through his research,

he discovered that the two men had become strikingly different from each other. One was happy, thriving, and clean-living; the other had become an alcoholic like his father and struggled with difficulties his entire life. The psychologist asked each of them why he had become the way he did, and each gave the same answer: "What else would you expect when you have a father like mine?"

The story demonstrates an important element implicit in stress, health, and human behavior. According to R. H. Schuller, "It is not what happens to you in life that makes the difference. It is how you react to each circumstance you encounter that determines the result."

Circumstances and genes do play a role in the quality of your life. But science shows that more than conditions or heredity, it's your choices that matter more. Just as the story of the two brothers demonstrates, it's the conclusions you make about who you are and what you're capable of as a result of your experiences that end up having the greatest positive or negative influence on your life.

Your mindset is the most influential operating system for your life. Wayne Dyer famously said, "Change the way you look at things, and the things you look at change." Spiritual life rests on the foundation of your ability to manage and refine your inner world – your thoughts, beliefs, emotions, perceptions, and energy. You can't stay the same and enjoy a new result.

Studies in positive psychology reveal that if a psychologist or scientist knew everything about your history and your current circumstances, they would still only be able to determine what would account for just ten percent of your long-term life satisfaction. Your overall happiness is actually predicted more by how your brain processes and interprets your life and the world around you. Science provides what spiritual masters have taught for thousands of years, which is that you don't see life as it is, you see life as you are.

While there are no guarantees on individual outcomes, I can say with complete sincerity that if you commit to applying the principles in this book with intention, faith, and consistency, you will experience a profound change in the way you experience yourself and life. You can create a new way of being that is happy, joyous, and free. Modern science and ancient wisdom agree that you have the capacity to retrain your mind, body, and nervous system and recreate your life. You are creative energy, cocreating your experience.

The seven spiritual principles detailed in this book are foundational elements of my Soul School coaching program, which I created after years of personal study, practice, and experience. It is a unique blend of yoga therapy, spiritual psychology, and positive psychology. I do not teach quick-fix solutions. Instead, I show spiritual seekers like you a real path for positive recreating and lasting change from the inside out. Remember, these are spiritual principles, not steps. Therefore, they are a design for living, rather than steps to take and check off your list. When applied, they can change your life, as they have for so many of my clients, and help you find your way back home to your inner confidence, wisdom, and joy. Personally, they have shaped the person I am today. It is the inner transformation that will set you free, not just the absence of anxiety. In the next seven chapters that follow, I will teach you how to live the seven foundational Soul School principles in your own life

The first principle will guide you toward your creative power. More than anything, it is your ability to positively influence your mindset that will change the quality of your life and help you solve anxiety. But your fears, doubts, and anxieties are also created in your mind. Your inner wisdom, clarity, and joy become covered by misperceptions, fears, and programming. So, the first principle is the starting point from which you will learn to reconnect to your inner truth and shape your life for new possibilities and outcomes by learning how to see the world and yourself in a new and empowering way.

The second principle involves clearing away negative thinking and misperceptions that limit your view of life and who you truly are. You've learned how to survive by trying to control life around you, but it has cost you your freedom and joy. In yoga psychology, misperception is the root of all suffering. Within this principle, you'll discover three core misperceptions that keep you stuck on the hamster wheel of anxiety and fear, and their antidotes. You'll learn a three-part process that will help you make decisions rooted in your truth and belief in yourself. This process will also enable you to cultivate discernment between your conditioned reality and your chosen reality. You'll step more fully into your role as a powerful and positive co-creator of your life.

Next, you'll discover the indispensable need for spiritual commitment, personal responsibility, and daily practice. This third principle is rooted in taking ownership of your life. Doing so is the only way to really rise above limiting circumstances, situations, or beliefs that perpetuate your anxiety. Everyone faces obstacles, but some people learn to turn them into opportunities. Change can be hard, but it is always possible. Here you'll be asked to make the number one decision that you must make as a spiritual seeker in order to move beyond your comfort zone and through the clunky stages of transformation, so you can finally untangle yourself from your fears and open yourself to your joy.

Yoga psychology defines visualization as the ability to see, feel, and experience your goal before it has happened. Through this fourth principle, you'll learn why becoming confident, calm, and joyful on the inside first is key to elevating your ability to change the patterns and conditioning of anxiety on a deep cellular level. This principle is a beautiful combination of spiritual effort and surrender.

When you live in a state of anxiety, you become trapped in a web of old habits and primal instinct; you are driven by autopilot rather than free will. But when you live in a state of faith, you're able to broaden your perspective, see the big picture and make new choices. You will more easily imagine positive outcomes and take new actions. In this fifth principle, I will present you with a process to determine your emotional state at any given moment and teach you how to establish more trust and faith in your daily life.

Some of the most profound work you will ever do to free yourself from anxiety is to surrender and forgive. This sixth principle is not for the weak but for the strong. It takes courage to let go of fear, resentment, or blame and open yourself up for more joy and fulfillment. Forgiveness is a byproduct of doing your own inner work and weeding out the triggers embedded in your mind, body, and heart. It is by letting go that you will experience the greatest freedom because you gain the space and energy to connect with your spiritual power.

Within the seventh principle is the deepest work of all. I will help you release the façade and protective layer that you have created to feel safe, but now just binds you tighter to your anxieties and fears. I will take you through a final process where you'll learn how to ground into the core of your being – your true self – and step fully into your chosen reality and identity, without the label of anxiety or the misperception of separateness from who you truly are.

As a spiritual seeker, these seven principles will probably not be new to you. But it is not the information that is as important as your commitment to apply them that matters.

Throughout this book, you will notice I sprinkle in words and concepts in Sanskrit, the dominant language of India. I will also give you the English translation, it's meaning, and importance. Often, I will reference *The Yoga Sutra*, the foundational text of yoga psychology.

You can download a PDF with the definitions of the Sanskrit words included in this book, along with an MP3 of audio pronunciation, for free at www.joystonecoaching. com/sanskrit.

Every great story has a hero, and every great hero eventually has a decision to make. Lauren made the decision to put her whole heart and energy into our work together. When I began coaching Lauren, her anxiety was at an all-time high. She was in a difficult marriage and was deeply unhappy. Lauren only stayed in her marriage because it was familiar. She was afraid of making a mistake, so she just stayed where she was. But her anxiety mounted. She couldn't see a way out. Anxiety limited her ability to open up to new positive outcomes for her future. Fear kept her from trusting herself. After three months of one-on-one coaching, Lauren left her marriage, moved to her dream city, and rented a new apartment. She felt more confident than she'd ever been. Lauren's life changed because she changed. What made the difference for Lauren, and for so many of my clients who have had similar experiences, was internalizing the process of becoming on the inside what she wanted to experience on the outside.

Adhikara is a beautiful Sanskrit word meaning spiritual authority. It is the expression, practice, and commitment to your studentship. It is the action of taking ownership of your life, specifically your inner life. *Adhikara* is essential as you become a spiritual student to the core, not just when it is convenient. This is the beginning of a wonderful new experience. I encourage you to embrace this spiritual experience with enthusiasm, curiosity, and an open heart.

Close your eyes, take a deep breath, and remember you are capable of great change and lasting joy.

CHAPTER 4:

Your Belief Window

"Your personality creates your personal reality."
— Joe Dispenza

Beliefs

As powerful as they can be, beliefs are not facts. They're just thoughts you've thought a lot. Your beliefs shape your reality because they frame how you see and experience anything and everything. Therefore, if you want a new experience, you will have to begin by creating new beliefs. In his book, *As a Man Thinketh*, James Allen wrote, "Men are anxious to change the circumstances of their lives but unwilling to change themselves."

In my twenties, I believed the biggest problem I had to solve was how to get over my difficult childhood. I blamed it for why I never felt worthy and became so anxious. I was obsessed with the question, "Why is life so unfair?" In therapy, I would ask this question over and over. I'd write endlessly about it in my journal. I wanted the answer to this problem.

This led me to the next nagging question of my life: "Why me?" I thought if I could solve the "Why me?" question, I'd magically feel better, and my confidence would be restored. But it was the belief that these questions had to be answered in order for me to feel better that kept me more imprisoned and made me more anxious.

One of the only benefits of questions like these is that they eventually make you so frustrated that you will gladly open your mind and heart to a new possibility. The belief that you have to solve every problem just produces a string of new problems and more pain. This habit can become a distraction to your freedom and joy.

For example, when the alcoholic continues to ask why she can't drink like the non-alcoholic, her life just becomes more complicated. She lives in resistance, trying to manage and control her drinking. In trying to solve her drinking problem, she creates other problems, and her life spirals out of control. But the real answer doesn't actually have anything to do with regulating her alcohol intake. In fact, the real answer seems to have nothing to do with the perceived problem at all; it's the surrender, admission, and willingness to look at her life from an entirely new perspective. But she can't see that because she believes she has to solve the *drinking* problem and goes on to experience more suffering.

When you lean toward anxiety, you tend to worry about the future and obsess about ways to control it. That is one of your biggest problems. You want to know what the outcome will be before you make a decision or take a step forward. You want to avoid any mistakes, failure, or loss. You ruminate and spin in mental circles. Just as your beliefs are not fact, your feelings aren't either. Emotions are simply chemical responses to what you think a lot. That's why you can still feel anxious even when you tell yourself you're okay. Your emotional body has developed the habit of producing stress hormones like cortisol and adrenaline to create the feeling of fear. For this reason, you not only have to practice thinking and believing differently but also feeling differently.

Whether it is alcoholism, anxiety, or any other flavor of suffering, it's the same. The answer ultimately lies within you. For that reason, you can't just take another deep breath, recite a new positive affirmation, or take another yoga class while you cling to old beliefs that reinforce your anxiousness. Freedom, confidence, and joy require your participation. They demand your willingness to become different on the inside.

In Sanskrit, *sat vata parinam vata* means "this is your reality, but your reality can change." It is necessary to acknowledge where you are and to have compassion for what you've been through, but you can't settle in with a tub of popcorn and fixate on it, not if you want to be free. To feel less anxious and live with more joy, you'll need to adjust your frequency and elevate your life to a new vibration from within. Albert Einstein said, "You can't solve your problems using the same kind of thinking you used when you created them." You are a powerful creator capable of transforming your reality because you *can* change what you think, believe, feel, and do. It is important to know that all change begins in the mind, which happens to also be exactly where anxiety arises.

Mahatma Gandhi said, "Your beliefs become your thoughts, your thoughts become your words, your words become your actions, your actions become your habits, your habits become your values, your values become your destiny."

What's important for you to internalize right now is that in order for you to transcend suffering, which is rooted in fear, you must take ownership of your *inner* life, starting with your beliefs and emotions. You'll also need to become invested for the long haul, not the quick fix. When you commit to your happiness and joy, the payoff is profound. Among other benefits, you'll restore your *prana*, Sanskrit for life-force energy. It is this life-energy that puts the sparkle in your eye, the skip in your step, the clarity in your mind, and the abundant well-being in your body. It is what you push out when you are anxious, afraid, and full of self-doubt.

Your Belief Window

In Chapter 3, I wrote that your mindset – what you think, believe, feel and imagine – is the most powerful operating system for your life. Moving forward, I will refer to this system as your belief window.

Your belief window has a filter – literally. Inside your brainstem is a group of neurons referred to in science as your reticular activating system. This filter is an evidence-finding machine. It doesn't care about truth or facts. Its job is to reflect back to you what you already believe. If you believe you have to worry about everything, this filter will look for evidence to prove you right and will ignore evidence to the contrary. In other words, it will bring more of what you already believe, not necessarily what you want, into your view, and therefore your life.

This is why just managing your anxiety triggers or trying to control conditions doesn't always work. You will just continue to experience the trigger if you keep your belief window as is. This is the science behind what you may have heard referred to as "the law of attraction" and why visualization and faith, which I will teach you more about in Chapter 7, are so important.

Mohini was a regal white tiger who lived for many years at the National Zoo in Washington, DC. She spent most of her time in an old twelve-by-twelve-foot lion cage with bars and a cement floor. The zoo desperately wanted to give Mohini a new home, one that represented her natural habitat. Biologists and zoo staff worked together and made it a reality. Her new home was expansive, with several acres of green grass, hills, trees, and ponds. With excitement, they released Mohini into her new space. But Mohini was conditioned. She settled into a corner of the environment where she remained for the rest of her life. She paced and paced, and over time, she wore a twelve-by-twelve-foot area into the grass.

Because of your reticular activating system and other conditioning, you, like Mohini, become a prisoner to your belief window, which you'll remember encompasses your programming, thoughts, imagination, memories, stories, emotions, anxieties, and fears. You become blind to a new life even when it's right there in front of you.

To further explain your belief window and how it influences your life, imagine three circles lined up horizontally. In yoga psychology, the circle on the left represents your soul, the circle in the middle represents your belief window or mindset, and the circle on the right represents the world.

Your soul circle, on the left, represents the part of you that is eternal, all-knowing, joyful, confident, and whole. It is the part of you that is totally free from self-doubt, uncertainty, anxieties, fear, and attachments. It's this part of you that is meant to be in the driver's seat of your life because it is your inner guidance system. Some people call this circle God, Purusha, Siva, Energy, Love, Source, Consciousness, or Universe. I will ask you later to give this circle a name that is meaningful and powerful to you.

Your belief window circle, in the middle, represents your mindset, or the lens you see the world through.

It gets clouded or blurry, and your vision becomes limited because of old residue left from past experiences, what we call *mala* in Sanskrit. Your belief window also stores everything you have ever created in your imagination about your past, present, or future and everything you already believe and feel. This circle is the place where all of your fears and anxieties, developed, what we call *vikalpa* in Sanskrit. As residue on your belief window builds, your soul circle gets blocked out, and suffering ensues.

Your world view circle, on the right, represents the world you see. The world does not look the same for any two people. Your world view circle reflects back to you what you are already projecting out from your belief window circle. Remember, life is happening *from* you, not to you. You always see the world as you are, not as it is. Anxiety and fear will only originate from this world view circle if you are in actual danger; otherwise, all of your fear and anxiety – which you often perceive as being caused by other people, places, and things – is being projected from your belief window or conditioning.

Think back to the personal story I shared about when I was thirteen and went to that school dance. At that time, I already believed I didn't belong. My belief window was projecting that impression onto the world I was seeing. For now, it doesn't matter how I developed that belief; it just matters that I had it. When that girl asked, "What are you doing here?" my belief window filter alerted me it had found evidence to prove my belief accurate. The

43

alarm went off inside of me: Ding! Ding! Ding! Your belief window is not concerned with facts or even with making you happy. Its job is simply to reflect back to you what you already believe.

If I believed differently, as I do now, that I am worthy just as I am, I could have responded differently to her remark. If that happened to me today, I might wonder in what way she was suffering that would cause her to hurt someone else. And yes, her remark would have stung, for sure. I would not spend time with her if I could avoid it. But the essential teaching here is that I wouldn't have had to suffer because I would not have internalized her words and believed them. They would not have triggered a wound or belief that was *already* taking up space inside of me.

If you're reading this and you're at all confused, don't worry. I promise, if you stay with me and go through this process, it will become clear.

Name Your Soul Circle

A central part of living with more trust and joy (and less anxiety) resides in your relationship with your soul circle, one that becomes core to your life and happiness. For now, consider and choose a name for your soul circle that is meaningful and powerful for you. Here are some examples: God, Universe, Seer, Love, Light, Peace, Joy, or Consciousness. Give your inner guide a name that resonates with you. Your relationship with who you truly are is essential to your healing and well-being.

On a piece of paper, write down everything you have believed, up to this point, about your soul circle. You will likely notice some of what you believe has been conditioned and defined for you by society, family or peers. You may notice that you are holding onto beliefs and ideas that don't ring true for you today. You might also discover you have beliefs about your soul circle that are blocking your joy, or sense of worthiness. Give yourself permission to let these go. Moving forward, you get to determine, decide and define what *you* believe.

Now, on a new piece of paper, write down what you want to believe about your soul circle. How do you choose to define this loving and all-knowing part of yourself? Think about how you want to feel in your life, then ask yourself, is your definition of your true nature, your soul circle, congruent with that desire? As you move forward in life, allow your relationship with your soul circle to be fluid, open and changeable. Your relationship with your soul circle will grow and develop, as you grow and develop.

In the words of the Swami Muktananda, the founder of Siddha Yoga, "For your spiritual development, all you need to know is your Self. If you get to know your Self, you will get to know everything. The first and foremost question is 'Who am I?' Everything else comes later. Self-discovery is the root of all actions, all duties, all religious practices. First, know your inner self."

What's on Your Belief Window?

Svadhyaya in Sanskrit means the practice of self-discovery, or spiritual reflection in order to understand and know your true self. You are *always* writing the story of your life. When you engage in earnest self-discovery, you will see yourself and your true nature from a different perspective, make positive changes, and learn to rewrite the story of your life.

Remember, your belief window, is where anxiety arises and gets stuck. I want you to practice *svadhyaya* by sitting quietly and writing down any reoccurring thoughts, emotions, beliefs, memories, or stories that show up on your belief window that limit you or activate anxiety and fear. Another way to do this is to journal for ten minutes in the morning and ten minutes at night. Just empty your mind onto the page. Look for themes in your writing; notice if the same thoughts, beliefs, fears, or stories come up more than once. This residue blocks the light of your courageous, confident, and joyful soul circle from shining forth in your life. The more your inner light is covered, the more your anxiety will increase. Here are some questions that will help you uncover mental and emotional residue:

- ▷ What are you most anxious about?
- ▷ What do you worry most about?
- ▷ Is there a feeling you struggle with again and again?
- ▷ Is there a dominant theme to your thoughts or beliefs that limit you?

▷ Where do you feel out of control in your life?

▷ What do you think about your future?

▷ What do you think you don't have enough of?

▷ Where do you avoid taking responsibility in your life?

▷ Why don't you take more risks in your life?

▷ How do you hide in your life?

▷ What negative opinions do you hold about yourself?

▷ Do you have any resentments?

▷ What or who do you avoid, and why?

▷ Is there someone you need to forgive?

▷ Is there something you feel guilty or ashamed about?

▷ What is your greatest fear?

▷ Did someone say or do anything in your past that hurt or limited your self-confidence? If so, what beliefs did you conclude about yourself because of it?

Next, answer these three questions:

▷ Which of your limiting beliefs have held you back the most?

▷ What have you missed out on in your life because of this belief?

▷ What would you gain if you changed this belief?

Whatever circumstances, or events that caused your current beliefs to form on your belief window often can't be undone. But the beliefs you have – the feelings, thoughts, and stories you concluded – *can* be changed. Remember, beliefs aren't facts. They are just thoughts, you've thought a lot. Your reticular activating system will always look for evidence to match what you already believe. As Swiss psychiatrist Carl Jung said, "Until you make the unconscious conscious, it will direct your life, and you will call it fate." Once you know what you're dealing with, you can begin to digest it, assimilate it, and eliminate what you don't need.

When Fran and I began working together she was incredibly anxious about her future. She felt like she was running in a never-ending circle of hopelessness, and was trapped in a lifestyle she didn't know how to get out of it. Her fear of the unknown, of letting people down, and of being judged, kept her from believing in a positive outcome for her future and from taking any action. Today, Fran is living a different life. Her life is changed, because her beliefs changed. Fran is joyful, free, and has made the changes she tried for years to make before we began our work together.

Everything Is Neutral

It's hard to believe – I know because I struggled with this one – but everything is neutral. That is not to say life doesn't mean anything. It simply means that our individual belief window gives everything we experience all of the meaning it has. There are 7.8 billion people on the planet and that equals 7.8 billion ways to see anything.

Remember the story of the two brothers in Chapter 3? They had the same exact childhood and two different outcomes. Each son created two completely different meanings out of the same neutral childhood. It was a terrible way to grow up, to be sure. But the point here is that each young man came to a different conclusion about who he would become.

Dispute Your Beliefs

On a piece of paper, write "A." "B." "C." "D." and "E." vertically.

- ▷ A is for Adversity or Activating Event. I want you to think of a recent or past adversity or challenge, something that caused you to feel anxious, worried or doubtful, or something that has clouded your belief window. Write it down on your piece of paper. Don't write about your beliefs or feelings just yet. Simply describe the situation and be as specific as you can. Include the who, what, when, and where. Once that is complete, move to the next letter.

- ▷ B is for Belief or Belief Window. Here is where you get to write out everything you believe about the adversity you listed previously. Write down what you were saying to yourself in the situation. Include as many thoughts as you can remember that were running through your mind. Be honest and just put it all down. Stick to just your thoughts, not feelings. Once that is complete, move to the next letter.

▷ C for Emotional Consequences. This is where you get to record the consequences or results of your beliefs. How do your beliefs – not the situation or event – limit you? How do they make you feel? How do you act when you believe or feel this way? List all of the emotions you feel, and as many reactions and behaviors as you can identify.

Pause and review what you've just written under adversity, beliefs, and consequences. Lean into the idea that everything is neutral. The adversity you wrote about has 7.8 billion possibilities for interpretation. It is your beliefs that drive the consequences or outcomes you experience. It is your belief about something that can liberate or imprison you. Change your beliefs and you change your life.

Think back to how I retold the story of going to that dance, or the story of the two brothers and how they took different paths. Remember that you can always learn to change the story inside of you and therefore change the way you see your entire life and your choices in it. Oprah said, "The smallest change in perspective can change a life."

Cross out the activating event section and the notes you made there. If you continue to argue or resist what is or has already happened, you will continue to believe more of what you already believe and feel more of what you already feel. Instead, turn your attention to section C. Look over the consequences you are experiencing in section C. Try to recognize that these are a result of your beliefs much more than the adversity itself. Within your beliefs is where you have the power to change this experience. Remember, you can't change the past, and you don't know what will happen in the future, but you can change how you see it and experience it. You can gain wisdom.

▷ D is for Dispute. I want you to challenge, or dispute, your beliefs. Be sure you don't dispute the adversity. Instead, point out the inaccuracies in your beliefs, or generate a more accurate or optimistic alternative belief about the adversity. I like to imagine how someone I love and admire would see the situation or me. What would they believe and say? Or, if it helps, finish this statement: "That's not completely true because..."

▷ E is for Energy. As you continue to practice this *svadhyaya*, you will begin to notice a lightness in your being. Your prana is being reestablished as you clear away residue from your belief window and allow the truth of your soul circle to shine through and guide your life.

You Are Always Worthy

Your worthiness is always a given. It's your belief in yourself that ebbs and flows. Too often, you stand on the inside of your belief window waiting for someone or something to come into view and reflect back to you your sense of security, or give you permission to stop carrying the weight of the world on your shoulders. But confidence is a decision you make and practice. It is a habit you cultivate. It is determined more by your belief in yourself than by your circumstances. When you develop faith in something bigger than your fear, confidence will grow. Trust is a core topic throughout this entire book. It is a pivotal tool within *The Yoga Sutra* and one I am committed to helping you nurture.

If you suffer or feel anxious at this moment, it does not mean anything is wrong with you. If you have been seeking solutions like I was and are still dealing with limiting beliefs, uncertainty, anxious thoughts, or fear, it doesn't mean you're doing anything wrong. I still have moments or days when I struggle. It is part of the human condition. Your mind likes to think in black and white, and that can block your progress. I want you to let yourself off the hook and take a deep breath. There are things in your life for which you have had no control over. Your programming runs deep, most of which was not implanted by you. So be kind to yourself on this journey. But, if you struggle for an extended period of time, what I want you to know is that there is a grace within the universe that offers you a way out. There is a way into a new experience; into deep joy and boundless confidence. You have just learned that you have the power and capacity to change your life and that you can be set free, and it all begins with your beliefs and your willingness to do the inner work.

CHAPTER 5:

Filling In Your Puzzle

"As you inquire into issues and turn judgments around, you come to see that every perceived problem appearing 'out there' is nothing more than a misperception within your own thinking."

—Byron Katie

I t turns out humans aren't very good at determining what will make them happy or unhappy. You tell yourself you'll feel less anxious when [blank] happens, or you need [blank] before you can feel content, happy, and secure. But the way your brain actually works is that if or when you get what you wish for, an entirely new set of requirements for your happiness will arise, and so on. If you don't get what you think you must have in order to feel happy, you've now placed your joy on the other side of something you may or may not have any influence over. This is what researchers call "affective forecasting."

Desires aren't wrong. Wanting something to be a certain way isn't the problem. Goals are good. But when your need for certainty is a requirement for joy and security, anxiety will persist. In an ever-changing world, what you have today may be gone tomorrow, and what you hope for now may take years to arrive. As the saying goes, "You can't control the wind, but you can learn to adjust the sails."

As you change the way you perceive life, your life changes; yoga calls this, *sat vata parinam vata*. However, it's not just your perceptions, and desires, that change, life itself is constantly changing too. Life is always more mystery than it is certainty. Every human experience is a complex journey of twists and turns, ups and downs, and triumphs and failures. The Yoga Sutra says that suffering will arise when you misperceive what is always changing – your belief window including everything you can see, taste, hear, feel, and touch - with what stays the same and is always steady – your soul circle and who you truly are deep inside. Your search for "enough-ness" and certainty in the constantly changing world around you causes you to lose sight of the stability and worthiness already present within you.

When you are in alignment with who you really are, you can't help but feel more stable and joyful. Therefore, if you want to feel less anxious, you have to become less anxious within your own being. Your soul circle is your steady, unchanging, and reliable, inner guidance system, which is divinely designed to lead you through this one precious life.

Changing and Changeless

To help you discern between what is always changing and what never changes, draw a vertical line down the middle of a piece of paper so that you have two sections. Title the section on the left side "changing" and the section on the right side "changeless." Together, these encompass the two aspects of your reality: one part moving and the other part stable.

> ▷ Changing represents everything in your physical world. It is all subject to change. This includes all of your internal experiences, such as emotions, mood, thoughts, feelings, beliefs, and memories. It also includes your physical body, relationships, and everything around you, including all of nature. Everything you experience through your five senses is always changing, in-motion, and impermanent. Everything on your belief window goes under this category. That is why one day, you can feel great, and the next feel overwhelmed.

> ▷ Changeless represents your unchanging inner self. This stable part of you is always present. It is synonymous with your soul circle from Chapter 4. This is your all-knowing and reliable inner guidance system. It is the only aspect of life that is permanent, consistent, and steady. This is the part of you that is meant to be leading the way.

Take a moment to reflect on your life. Fill in the "changing" side of your grid with everything you can think of that is either changing or has changed. Remember change is inevitable. Notice which changes bring up fear or anxiety. Also, notice where you are projecting fear or anxiety onto your future.

On the "changeless" side, write down the name you gave your soul circle from the last chapter. Then, honestly rate the quality of your connection to this changeless part of you on a scale from one to ten, with ten being high. The higher your rating and greater your connection to your true self – what, in yoga, is called *samadhi* – the less active your anxieties and fears become. They are in an intimate proportionate relationship with each other.

Filling in Your Puzzle

Imagine life is a ten thousand-piece puzzle. You have just three pieces, but you think you have the entire puzzle. The other 9,997 pieces of the puzzle – which is constantly changing – get filled in with your personal belief window, including your, imagination, expectations, and a little bit of what you don't even know you don't know. Your puzzle only is filled in and exists in this particular way in your mind. No one else on the planet sees your puzzle – life – exactly as you do, and you don't see any other puzzle in the same way that the creator of another puzzle does. We all have a puzzle, and we all think we have all the pieces.

When you become attached to how your puzzle must look, or you develop an aversion to other puzzles, you will run into conflict and more anxiety. Thoughts, positive or negative, are a function of your ability to form a reality that hasn't happened yet. Anxiety is the habit of creating a negative reality. Through your anxious imagination, you will create a puzzle, filled in with, worst-case scenarios and catastrophic outcomes. Your future doesn't actually exist in this moment. It is a puzzle put together in your mind. When you fill in the uncertain, and constantly changing gaps with fear, more anxiety is produced; uncertainty, indecision, and doubt will arise and keep you stuck.

The Five Negative States of Mind

The Yoga Sutra describes this process of filling in the puzzle as the *kleshas*. These five negative states of mind are the root cause of human suffering and anxiety.

1. *Avidya* means misperception or not seeing clearly. The main misperception and primary cause of your anxiety is your inability to discern between your habitual thoughts and emotion with who you truly are – your soul circle.

2. *Asmita* means false identification. It's when you conflate what you do, the things you have or don't have, and the many roles you play in life with your worth. This causes anxiety because your sense of

security and joy becomes conditional on your ability to control what always changes.

3. *Raga* means attachment or clinging. Here, you are pulled by your need for life to go a certain way and for people to behave in a particular way for you to be happy. Here, you become attached to your comfort zone and find a false sense of security in what is familiar, even when those things or behaviors don't make you happy or move you forward. For example, when there is no real reason in your environment to be anxious, your mind simply attaches to anxiety-producing thoughts and therefore becomes a source of suffering.

4. *Dvesa* means avoidance. You become hyper-focused on what you don't like, don't want, and won't change. Avoidance not only produces more anxiety, but it also fuels anger and jealousy. Your world becomes small, and you will feel increasingly fearful and stuck.

5. *Abhinivesa* is the fear of not being able to survive, not only to survive physically but also the anxiety that you won't have what you need now or in the future. You're afraid to let go of a story of who you think you are, and you become anxious about whether you are good enough, pretty enough, or smart enough to thrive, be loved, and be successful.

Psychiatrist Daniel G. Amen has named the limiting thoughts we hear in our head "ANTs," automatic negative thoughts. Just like real ants at a picnic, your ANTs can ruin your experience of life.

Traditionally, you've been taught to think, "My anxiety causes me to worry and to have negative thoughts." But consider looking at it this way, "I'm prone to negative thinking (the five *kleshas*), therefore, I am anxious." Notice how this slight difference in perspective places the power to transform your life, and be free, back in your hands.

One of the first things I help my clients with when we begin working together is to clean up their mental and emotional habits by committing to a thirty-day practice of no blaming, judging, criticizing, or complaining.

When Michelle and I began working together, she blamed her ex-husband for what she perceived was wrong with her life. She felt angry, resentful, unhappy, and anxious. I taught Michelle that playing victim keeps people stuck because it blocks them from taking responsibility for their lives, which is necessary to reclaim confidence and joy. The hurdle, though, is that blaming can feel safe and comfortable because it keeps you from having to do the uncomfortable work of changing and growing.

Through our coaching together, Michelle became aware that her fear of feeling judged, unworthy, and abandoned caused her to stay passive in her relationship with her husband. She became accommodating and agreeable to everything he wanted. Over the years, she'd become more anxious and less confident to express her needs and ideas. By helping Michelle apply the principles in this book and be more deliberate with her thoughts, words, choices, and actions, she was able to take ownership where she'd been blaming. Michelle shifted her life in an entirely new direction. Today she is happy, confident, and reconnected to her soul circle – her inner guidance system.

Challenge yourself to thirty days of no complaining or blaming. When you notice yourself complaining, instead, stomp those automatic thoughts out by repeating this simple mantra, "Peace begins with me." You will quickly become aware of how much you were complaining and blaming before. This mindfulness will help you see what's possible when you try to fill in your puzzle with more positive and empowering thoughts, beliefs, interpretations, and solutions.

My Awakening to New Puzzle Pieces

I watched from my car as people were going in and out of the grocery store. I tried to stop crying just long enough to go in. It was my birthday, and I felt anxious. Recent changes in my personal life had triggered intense self-doubt and fear. Layered into my anxiety was an immense frustration about feeling so rattled. I'd done all the "spiritual things" to feel better, so why was I still so anxious? I had hit a new bottom, a level of surrender I'd never experienced before.

Moments later, I felt the anxiety lift. A profound sense of calm and peace came through me. I stopped crying and suddenly knew anxiety was not the problem I had to solve. I'd been filling in my puzzle with the wrong diagnosis. It was this subtle yet profound shift in my perception that became the catalyst for the joy I experience today.

The following *three misperceptions about anxiety* summarize the awakening I had that day in my car. These are the same spiritual rearrangements and mindset shifts I help my clients understand, discern, and experience. As they do, the results are tangible and profound. It's necessary for you to know, and internalize, that it is your lack of clarity, negative thinking, and disconnection from your soul circle– the way you fill in your puzzle – that will cause you to continue to fall victim to the cycle of thinking, believing, perceiving, and feeling that will only perpetuate your anxiety. In yoga, this is called *dukkha*, or suffering. Conversely, clarity is the turning point that, when cultivated, will bring you tremendous *sukha*, ease, and joy.

Misperception Number One: Symptom or Diagnosis?

Disconnection from your soul circle is the universal human diagnosis. It is the ultimate cause of suffering. Every form of dis-ease is a symptom of this one diagnosis. When you are mentally, emotionally, or spiritually disconnected from your soul circle, you will suffer. You experience this diagnosis of disconnection in the form of a *symptom,* called anxiety. Others may experience the diagnosis of spiritual disconnection with symptoms such as depression, loneliness, an eating disorder, drug or shopping addiction, alcoholism, and codependency.

You hold your deepest fears tight inside, hoping no one will find out. But that only builds a wall between you and your inner guidance system. You live under the misperception that if you work harder on managing your anxiety, you'll find the comfort and freedom you seek. But because life always changes, your strategy won't work. Something will always come along to upset your plan. It's like trying to grasp at air. You can't catch it, so it just breeds more frustration and anxiety.

When you reconnect to who you truly are instead of trying to solve the wrong problem, your life will radically change.

Misperception Number Two: Pattern or Person?

You are never going to be more spiritual than you are right now. You are always part of spirit. You are, at your core, your soul circle. Trying to control anxiety with more spiritual tools when you are misperceiving who you are won't work. From this viewpoint, your focus is still on the symptom relief, not the solution.

Anxiety is a pattern in your mind and body, what in yoga, is called, *samskara*. Anxiety is not who you are. It is a mental misperception, a physiological habit, and a spiritual misalignment. You most certainly have a personal history, a constitution, a predisposition, and an experience that has set the anxiety ball rolling in your life, but the point here is that your true nature is not anxious. It is a human pattern that you have developed in your mind and body, and it can be changed.

Misperception Number Three: Failure or Feedback?

Anxiety is not failure, it's feedback. If you're not in danger, then anxiety is valuable feedback about what is happening *within* you. First, when you're anxious, one or more of the five negative mental states – the *kleshas* – are active. If you take action while in that state, you could end up suffering more. Second, and most importantly, anxiety is showing you where you are in your relationship with your soul circle and true self. Anxiety is powerful feedback that can help you navigate your life with more mastery.

Everything is a reflection of your relationship with your inner being. Think of your emotions as an inner navigation system, and there are only two directions in which your emotions can take you: toward fear or toward love. Anxiety is immediate feedback that you are moving in the direction of more fear, and that you must turn around and go back home – toward love. It is your connection with your soul circle that will set you free and allow you to experience more joy.

Discernment

Discernment, what *The Yoga Sutra,* calls *viveka*, is what you will experience as you clear away the misperceptions and negative states of mind that are blocking you from your soul circle. When you're able to discern between what is changing and what is changeless, you will not only reduce your current anxiety but also avoid future suffering. The bottom line is, if you are suffering, you need more discernment.

The only way for you to cultivate more discernment is to practice discernment. To begin, try this simple "labeling your thoughts" meditation. This will help you experience more space between you and your automatic thoughts. Viktor Frankl famously said, "Between stimulus and response there is a space. In that space is your power to choose your response. In your response lies your growth and your freedom." The more space you can create between your changing thoughts (stimulus) and your response (kleshas) the more power (discernment) you will have.

Close your eyes. Breathe in and out through your nose. Pay attention to your breath as it moves in and out through your nostrils. Make your inhalations slow and deep. Make your exhalations long and smooth. Continue to breathe in and out through your nose for several minutes. Then, as you become aware of a thought, simply label it, by silently saying, "this is just a thought" and turn your attention back to your breath flowing in and out of your nostrils. Continue this simple mindfulness meditation for several minutes. Repeat daily and as needed throughout the day.

Questions are another powerful way to develop more discernment. By framing any situation with a solution-focused question instead of a problem-focused question you can unlock new positive possibilities, perspectives, outcomes and opportunities for spiritual growth. Here are five of my favorite questions:

> ▷ What is the spiritual lesson in this for me?
> ▷ What are the facts of this situation and where am I making assumptions based on those facts?
> ▷ Where do I have choice in this situation or circumstance?
> ▷ What am I willing to think, feel, believe or do differently to make things more the way I want them to be or have an experience I prefer?
> ▷ Is this where I want to focus my attention and energy right now?

The 3 S Process

It is also important that you learn to tune in and listen to your inner guidance system. When I was in the travel industry, people would often tell me how much they'd love to have my job. From the outside, it seemed almost perfect. I got to travel the world, experience new adventures, and meet wonderful people. Yet, I wanted to do other things. At the time, I knew I wanted to teach yoga. Unfortunately, I lacked the ability to discern between my need for approval and what I wanted. The fact that other people liked my job caused me to doubt myself. I was disconnected from my soul circle and looked for assurance and answers from the people around me. The problem was everyone had a different opinion, and therefore I just got more anxious and more stuck. Can you relate?

When I'm helping my clients make positive, clear, and confident decisions, I always teach them the 3 S Process. It is an empowering reflection that will turn your attention toward extracting wisdom from your inner guidance system and away from approval-seeking and anxiety.

Get in the habit of using this process when making decisions, from small to big. It will help you cultivate discernment, develop your ability to see a new possibility for yourself, take new actions, and be led by your soul circle, rather than by fear or anxiety.

On a piece of paper, draw two lines horizontally across your paper so that you end up with three equal-sized sections. Title the top section *Sri*, the middle section *Satya*, and the bottom section *Svatantrya*.

▷ The first section, *Sri*, is Sanskrit for life-affirming. Is your decision life-affirming for you? Will this choice bring you more balance, harmony, or joy, or will it not? Is it aligned with your heart, vision, and intentions? Does it make you feel more inspired or depleted?

▷ The middle section, *Satya*, is Sanskrit for truth. Is your choice true for you? Is it an old pattern, habit, or fear driving your decision, or is it the best decision for you at the current time? Are you making this choice just to please others? Is it aligned with your truth or the direction you want to go in life?

▷ The bottom section, *Svatantrya*, is Sanskrit for freedom-enhancing. Does this decision make you feel freer or more in bondage? Will it bring you immediate gratification but cause more long-term pain? Are you saying yes to something in the moment because it's easier than setting a boundary? Are you choosing to remain in your comfort zone even though making a new choice could lead you to more joy?

There is no need to work hard at solving your problems because you're almost always trying to resolve the wrong ones anyway. When you clear away the cobwebs of misperception and negative thinking, you will realize that the wisdom of your soul circle has been there all along. You are not here to face and endure an anxious reality; you are here to create a joyful one.

CHAPTER 6:

No One Is Coming

---

*"Freedom is not the absence of commitments,
but the ability to choose and commit myself to
what is best for me."*

—Paulo Coelho

Discovering New Puzzle Pieces

My husband and I were driving home from the beach when I received the call. It was my dad's ex-wife.

"Joy, you need to come home right away," she said. "Your dad's in the hospital in critical condition."

I lived in California, and my dad was in Seattle. We hadn't spoken in a long time. In fact, I'd been with my husband for five years, and my dad had never even met him.

He was in the ICU and unconscious when I arrived. His head had been shaved to accommodate the emergency surgery from the brain aneurysm. Tubes and machines were everywhere. Nurses were in and out. I was terrified of seeing my dad like that and afraid of my emotions.

A dear friend who lived in Seattle agreed to meet me. She stood next to my dad's bed when I walked into his hospital room, my heart pounding out of my chest. I held his hand and told him I was there. For the first time in years I said, "I love you, Dad."

I remember being in awe at how many people came to see my father. Friends shared stories about his generosity and kindness, and described him as gentle, humble, and warm. People exchanged memories of times when my dad gave them a place to stay, money for food, or a job so they could pay their bills. The visitors continued for days and the stories of his thoughtfulness seemed endless. Almost every one of them would say, "You're Joy. He talks about you all the time. He's so proud of you." I saw my dad through their eyes.

I thought I knew everything I needed to know about my dad. I assumed I had all the puzzle pieces. I told myself it was okay that I shut him out because he abandoned me first. Sometimes we put people in categories and keep them there. But in the process, you stay stuck too. My teachers' words were ringing in my ears: "Allow other people the right to change."

My aunt told me about the abuse and neglect he endured as a child: the beatings, humiliations, and mental cruelty. My heart hurt for him. I realized then that my dad hadn't chosen alcohol over me, as my nine-year-old self had believed; he was desperately trying to numb out his suffering. His belief window had been clouded with his fears, conditioning, and projections. I was humbled. My dad was human. He wasn't immune to the disconnection that causes you or me to sometimes suffer. Here I was finding out that life is not black or white. Life is a million shades of grey.

You Always Have a Choice

In an article, Pema Chodron, an American Tibetan Buddhist, shared a profound story of when she was six years old and took a walk. She felt lonely, unloved, and mad, kicking anything she could find. A woman watching said to her, "Little girl, don't you go letting life harden your heart." Many years later, Pema would teach the world that "You can let the circumstances of your life harden you so that you become increasingly resentful and afraid, or you can let them soften you and make you kinder and more open to what scares you." You always have this choice.

For a long time afterward, I let the circumstances, conditions, and experiences of my childhood harden me. My resentments, anger, and anxiety became like a little prison. Fear cut me off from the love, joy, and safety of my soul circle. What happened to me when I was young was wrong. I was not responsible for the actions of my parents, but I was responsible for how I would allow those things to make me feel, think, and believe moving forward. If my dad died, all that suffering inside of me would remain because I nurtured it. You can't selectively numb one

71

area of your life without dimming your entire light. What you can't emotionally and mentally digest will eventually disturb your *prana* and create dis-ease, such as anxiety.

The Most Important Relationship Is the One You Have with Your Self

Nathanial Brandon, a psychotherapist known for his work in the psychology of self-esteem, concluded from his research that one of the strongest pillars of self-esteem is taking personal responsibility. You will take responsibility for your life when you truly internalize that no one is coming to save you. There are things in life that only you can do for yourself. It turns out setting yourself free is one of them.

Your spiritual path requires you to take ownership of your life. You are capable of overcoming great obstacles when you stop focusing on them. You are either expanding or contracting at any given moment. The longer you avoid the discomfort of growth, the more you contract, and ultimately, the more pain you will feel. You are free to continue your habit of thinking negatively, blaming, creating worst-case scenarios, and reiterating all the reasons why you can't change, but if you do, anxiety will remain. The longer you go on in the direction of trying to avoid pain, the harder it will be to change direction.

It may not be easy, and it may not be overnight, but you can mold your life toward more confidence, joy, and peace. Just as a plant will lean toward the sun, your inner light is always moving toward you. Your soul circle wants to shine through and lead the way.

One of the reasons you suffer is because your mind remains fixated on the things that scare you and on the things you can't change. Jim Rohn said, "Getting and becoming are like Siamese twins. If you want more than what you've got, you have to become more than who you are." When my dad was in the hospital, I faced some big fears. I didn't push them away even though part of me wanted to. Instead, I chose to look them in the eye, and I began the spiritual process of extracting lessons, gaining wisdom, and surrendering what I could no longer bear to hold.

Yoga does not deny that bad things will happen. It doesn't teach you how to avoid pain – that's impossible. Instead, it provides you a way out of suffering. Sometimes it's through your most difficult experiences – the darkness – that you finally find yourself.

Years ago, I came across a woman's obituary. She was from Seattle, my hometown, so it sparked my interest. She had terminal cancer and wrote a beautiful message to her daughters before she died. In it, she wrote, "I love you so much, and I'm so proud of you. I wish you such good things. May you, every day, connect with the brilliancy of your own spirit. And may you always remember that obstacles in the path are not obstacles, they are the path."

My client, Sarah, struggled with debilitating self-doubt. It was an obstacle she allowed to limit her happiness for years. Sarah worried about what other people thought about her. She became enmeshed, codependent, and people-pleasing in her personal and work relationships. Sarah felt guilty whenever she tried to set a boundary. This type of fear is common in people who struggle with anxiety. It is rooted in the misperception that your worthiness or "enough-ness" must be earned, and therefore, can be taken away. Through our work together Sarah got honest with herself. She took ownership of her life by taking responsibility for her thoughts, beliefs, feelings, and actions. Together, we discerned her truth and created a new reality for her life. She took action and surrendered the limiting habit of blaming external factors for her anxiety. By changing herself, Sarah was able to break anxious habits that had been with her for decades. She began our work together hoping to relieve her anxiety, but instead found freedom and joy. Sarah is a new person today because she did the inner work.

You won't be for everyone in this world. Not everyone will like you. But the most important question you can ask is, "Do you love who you are?" The approval addiction, which is almost always active in people with anxiety, is toxic. It's an addiction born out of fear. And like most fears, the *fear* of not being liked is worse than the reality of it. By being who you truly are and living your life honestly, you will find the right people, and they will find you. You are here to write your story; to be the hero in the book of your life.

Rising above Circumstances and Habits

Through my positive psychology program, I learned about the work of Marva Collins. She was a schoolteacher in the 1970s in the inner-city area of Chicago, an environment she described was filled with violence, drugs, and more than anything, hopelessness. Most teachers had resigned to their students' inevitability of living a life of gangs and crime.

Marva Collins had a different vision. She brought a message of hope to kids who had none, and she followed it up with action. She told them, "We're going to do a lot of believing in ourselves here." She would tell them, "I believe in you," "I know you can do well," and "I expect a lot from you." Marva Collins told her young students, "We're going to take responsibility for our lives." She didn't ask them to deny their conditions; she taught them how to develop a new empowering belief system, vision, trust, and commitment so they could thrive in spite of their environment. Amazing things happened for the kids Marva Collins taught and mentored. Thousands of students who had been written off as "unteachable" were able to lead meaningful, productive lives because one woman refused to give up on them and taught them how to take responsibility for their lives.

Habits, like anxiety, run deep. Therefore, the potency of your practice will be in direct proportion to the level of your commitment and faith, not in how many downward-facing dogs you can do. I remember years ago hearing the story of two men swimming across a lake. At the center of the lake was a small piece of land where they decided to take a rest. After a few minutes, Man Number One was ready to get back in the water and continue his swim to the other side. Man Number Two felt overwhelmed and unsure, so he chose to swim back to where they started. It was the same distance either way. That's the power of your comfort zone and your habits. Your reactions become automatic. Justifications and rationalizations become a human way of life. You cling to your familiar puzzle even when it's not better or easier, even when there is evidence to the contrary.

My dad lived for another twelve years after his stroke. My gratitude for those years is immense. We were graced with time to get to know each other. We laughed, cried, argued, and faced as much challenge as we did joy. We grew as individuals together in ways we couldn't have alone. I was able to change the pattern within myself to run away and avoid the hard stuff. My dad was able to shed guilt and shame and address his fear of not being good enough. We had a meaningful and real relationship that lasted until the moment he died on March 18, 2019. On March 9, nine days before he passed, I received this text from my dad: "With all the people I know with daughters, no one has a daughter that comes close to having the love and compassion that you have. I mean that with all of my heart." I am so grateful I didn't miss the person my dad was and the love he had to give.

Expanding Your Comfort Zone

The more you expand beyond your comfort zone, the more discomfort you will feel. I want you to know that this is normal. In yoga, this stage of growth is called *vitarka*, because it is clunky and awkward. But it is your aversion to this unfamiliar place and your haste for immediate results that will cause you to go back to your comfort zone, not the discomfort itself. If you commit and you're willing to be uncomfortable for a while, you will soon find your way to a new and liberating state of being. You will notice yourself thinking, feeling, and acting in positive new ways. Things will become easier and easier for you. New habits and beliefs will be established and become your new default. Triggers may sometimes still flare-up, and anxieties may arise, but your decision to take responsibility for the quality of your life will empower you to observe even those moments from a new vantage point. Your belief window will be cleaner and clearer; you'll be immersed in a renewed relationship with your soul circle. This is yoga.

Viktor Frankl, the author of *Man's Search for Meaning*, wrote, "When you are no longer able to change a situation, you are challenged to change yourself."

The next time you encounter a situation or challenge that triggers your pattern of anxiety, pause instead and ask yourself, "Can I accept this experience as it is? Can I change my perception of the situation? Or is it necessary to leave the situation, to set a boundary, or to do both?"

Taking personal responsibility is not blaming yourself. It is having the courage to change what you can change. Yoga Sutra 1:1 *atha yoganusasnum* states, "Now is the time for yoga." This means if you are suffering, now is the time to clear away the misperceptions that are contributing to your anxiety and discover who you truly are.

Will you commit?

CHAPTER 7:

Everything Is Created Twice

"Only one who devotes himself to a cause with his whole strength and soul can be a true master. For this reason, mastery demands all of a person."

—Albert Einstein

A New Belief Window

Do you believe that life is essentially good or bad? Albert Einstein famously said, "The most important decision you will make is whether you believe you live in a friendly or hostile universe." In Chapter 4, you learned you have a filter in your brain that causes you to see more of what you already believe, not necessarily what you want. Visualization, which is called *bhavana* in Sanskrit, is how you begin to reprogram your belief window by creating a new vision and positive story for your life. Visualization changes you, and then it changes the world you see.

Hebbs Law, a scientific discovery, states, "Neurons that fire together, wire together." This means what you repeatedly think, feel, believe, and do becomes grooved into your nervous system until you unconsciously fall into the same behaviors, thoughts, and choices day after day. It's why you don't have to think about brushing your teeth, tying your shoe, or driving your car. You've done those actions so many times that now you do them without thinking. Those memorized actions make your life easier and more efficient. Can you imagine waking up every morning having to relearn the skills you mastered the day before?

But what about the skills you've mastered that make your life harder? What about the habitual thoughts, beliefs, emotions, and behaviors that cause you to suffer? Anxiety in the absence of an actual threat means your body has developed the habit of replaying and reproducing the same thoughts and chemicals that result in the same anxious reaction again and again. Anxiousness has become automatic, just like tying your shoe or brushing your teeth.

William James, the father of American psychology, said, "The greatest discovery of my generation is that a human being can alter his life by altering his attitudes." Through the practice of visualization – combined with commitment and trust– you can retrain your "attitude" by reprogramming your reticular activating system to filter different experiences into your reality. You can create new habits – *samskaras* – in your nervous system, rewrite your story, and change your default thoughts, beliefs, emotions, and chemical reactions.

The success of yoga isn't measured in your ability to touch your toes or stand on your head. *The Yoga Sutra* says success lies in your capacity to settle your mind and give up your addiction to thinking in the same way day after day. Ninety percent of yoga practice – or spiritual practice – is the ongoing cleaning up of your internal accumulations, such as the misperceptions, attachments, aversions, fears, and projections that can block you from experiencing your true confidence and joyful nature.

For example, if you wear glasses, you don't just clean them once and never clean them again. You most likely clean your glasses several times a day so you can continue to see clearly. The same is true for your belief window. And the same is true for your vision of happiness and well-being. You have to see it to experience it.

Faith

That is why *shraddha* is the indispensable first tool of *The Yoga Sutra*. Translated from Sanskrit as faith, conviction, or belief, *sraddha* is the belief you have in your new vision; it helps you build the capacity to do something today you couldn't do yesterday. While visualization is the actual practice of imagining on the inside the vision of yourself and your life that you want to experience, *shraddha* is your conviction in that vision. Without a strong conviction in your new way of being – how you want to think, believe, feel, and act – you won't let go of where you are right now. Faith is the belief that when you let go, you will be supported.

Visualization is not a wish for something better; it's the cultivation of new thoughts, beliefs, emotions, and images that will help you retrain your reticular activating system and reshape what you see when you look out into the world. In other words, you commit to becoming on the inside what you want on the outside. And the more vividly you can internally experience your desired outcome, the nearer you are to it. This is the creative energy of visualization and the power of faith.

Jesus said, "Seek, and you shall receive according to your faith." He didn't say, "Seek, and you shall receive according to what you beg or hope for." He said you will find what you have faith that you will find. Jesus was healing the sick because he had one hundred percent faith in wellness. He wasn't focused on trying to make people less sick; he was helping people experience their wholeness. He said that you too can do what I do.

The Bhagavad Gita is an ancient Indian text featuring the relationship between Arjuna and Krishna. Krishna represents your soul circle or higher self. Arjuna represents your belief window and the world you live in. Krishna finds Arjuna anxious and afraid over a difficult decision he must make. Arjuna's mind is overcome with anxiety and fear, and he wants to give up. Krishna reminds Arjuna that he is suffering because he's put his faith and focus in the wrong place. Like Arjuna, you have to untangle yourself from the misperceptions, attachments, and aversions that are causing your anxiety. To free yourself, you too must embrace a new perspective, look toward your soul circle, and master the principles of faith and visualization.

Visualization

Marva Collins helped her students visualize something better than their conditions might have permitted. In every way, every day, she taught them how to develop their faith in their future. She wasn't trying to fix them; she was helping them build an entirely new foundation from which to live their lives.

Visualization and faith are what made the difference between Man Number One swimming across the lake to the other side and Man Number Two going back where he started. Man Number One saw himself getting to the other side of the lake. He believed he could do it. Man Number Two saw himself going back to his comfort zone. Remember, it was the same distance. Their individual vision and faith determined their direction. You can visualize the best for your future, or you can picture the worst scenarios and outcomes.

Imagine the universe as a ball of playdough. Decide what you want to create with this piece of playdough. Close your eyes and visualize your hands molding the dough into the shape you imagined. Did the playdough resist and try to become another shape? The point here is, you're molding your life all day long with your thoughts, beliefs, emotions, and actions, and the universe won't argue with you. You can choose to focus on the uncertainty of a situation, or you can learn something from it. You can choose to blame, or you can take responsibility. You can choose to look backward, or you can look forward.

On May 8, 1954, Roger Banister was the first human on record to run a mile under four minutes, coming in at three minutes and 59.4 seconds. Until that moment, the belief of most medical professionals and athletes was that it was impossible to run a mile in less than four minutes. But Roger Banister did not let that deter him from visualizing something else. He didn't just believe it; he put his heart and soul into it. His ability to see beyond what people said was impossible had a ripple effect. On June 21, 1954, just six weeks later, John Landy beat Banister's record, coming in at three minutes 57.9 seconds. Since then, more than five hundred men have gone on to beat the record, with the current fastest time of three minutes 43 seconds held by Hicham El Guerrouj.

Knowledge versus Transformation

When I was thirty-eight years old, one of my dearest friends in the whole world unfriended me. Not on social media but in real life. To this day, there was no explanation, just an abrupt end. All the information about *samskaras* and *mala* didn't save me. Understanding that we each see life through a belief window didn't comfort me. The situation devastated me, and my entire world felt like it went dark. This may sound dramatic, but it was my experience. It was as if I was thirteen years old and back at that school dance. "I don't belong. I'm not loveable. Something is wrong with me." Those were the thoughts running through my mind over and over. I was suffering.

At that point in my spiritual evolution, I was an information gatherer. I loved to read, learn, and memorize teachings. I was a dedicated student and practitioner, but I was mistaking knowledge for transformation. I had a lot of awareness, and I'd come a long way, but I hadn't established the inner resiliency, confidence, and self-love I have today. I didn't fully digest the idea that my spiritual practices were only there to support me in making changes within myself. I didn't understand that the practices were not the solutions in and of themselves.

Nine years later, I experienced a similar loss. My reaction was different. I could still feel the twinge of pain from the residue of my earlier experiences, but my new beliefs had become bigger and stronger than the old ones. For the last decade, I'd been committed to doing the inner work. I'd visualized – internally seen, felt, and believed – new outcomes for myself and my life. I'd taken new actions and wired a new life for myself from the inside out.

You can't control whether someone will decide to leave or stay – or anything in the ever-changing world around you – but you can choose not to suffer. You don't struggle in life because you don't have what you want or because something changes, you suffer because you believe you need whatever it is to feel good again, and that belief creates distance between you and your soul circle.

Everything is created twice. Stephen Covey, the author of *Seven Habits of Highly Effective People*, writes, "There's a mental or first creation and a physical or second creation to all things."

Smriti is a Sanskrit word that means memory or recollection. It's not the memory of a past experience but instead the remembering of a new vision until it is absorbed in your mind, body, and heart – what, in yoga, is called *samadhi* – or complete union with your goal. This special kind of memory, *smriti*, is an essential element in the practice of faith and visualization. Your imagination doesn't know the difference between something that is happening in your mind or in actual life. This means you can wire new *samskaras* or neural pathways, noted in Hebb's law, by creating new memories and new experiences in your imagination. You can visualize your new reality. And the more you do, the more you will expect it, and the more you expect it, the more you will take new actions that move your life in an entirely new direction; one that is mapped out by your inner confidence, wisdom, and joy, not your fear.

Gratitude and Joy

Gratitude and joy are currents of creative energy. *Ananda* is a Sanskrit word that means bliss. As you practice gratitude and joy, you will settle more into the creative vibration of bliss. *Ananda* is a kind of love or energy that knows no opposite. It's not something you analyze with your mind, but something you lean into and experience. The presence of bliss is the absence of fear, doubt, and anxiety. And the more you live in this energy, the more you expand into your ability to choose, and to create, and experience your true nature, which is confidence and joy.

After you wake up and before you go to sleep, move your body for a few minutes by doing yoga or stretching. This is a wonderful way to destress your body and prepare your mind for meditation. Then, when you feel ready, sit with your spine upright in a comfortable seat and place your hands over your heart. Breathe in and out through your nose. Soften your eyes, relax your jaw, and create a slight smile on your face. Breathe in the feeling of gratitude. Rather than listing the things you appreciate, try to embody the sense of gratitude. Let your heart expand as you simply appreciate what is good in your life. Then, after a few minutes of gratitude and appreciation, place your hands on your lap and relax. Next, focus your attention on the joy within your being – your soul circle. When your mind wanders, simply guide it back to your breath and the joy within you. Let the feelings of gratitude and joy increase and expand throughout your entire body. Turn your mouth upwards to a slight smile and keep your eyes soft. Imagine your whole body smiling.

Visualize Your Way Into Your Day

In the morning, after your movement and *Ananda* meditation, practice the following visualization exercise. With your eyes closed, consider your day ahead of you. Bring to mind all of your to-dos, such as family commitments, work obligations, leisure activities and self-care practices. As you imagine your day, continue to breathe in and out through your nose and stay relaxed in your body. See yourself going through your day with ease. Notice anything about the day ahead that would normally cause you to feel anxious or doubtful. See yourself handling those situations with confidence and peace. Notice how you talk, stand, and walk when you feel confident. See yourself as happy and joyful. Stay in your vision for several minutes, or until it feels real.

A New Way to End Your Day

The moments just before you fall asleep and just as you wake up are some of your most powerful creative moments. During these transitions, your brain is vibrating at the theta brain wave level. While in the theta state, the subconscious mind is more open, accessible, and receptive to new programming and new seeds of possibility. You are bypassing the monkey mind and accessing the part of your brain which stores your habits, and which you can learn to consciously and positively program. In the evening, after your movement and *Ananda* meditation, I encourage you to read one of my favorite evening meditations – one I share with all of my coaching clients – called "The First Meditation" from U. S. Anderson's book, *Three Magic Words*. Simply read it right before you turn out your light. Let it be the last thing you feed your subconscious before you go to sleep. You will find a copy of this reading meditation in the appendix of this book.

Just like the great spiritual teachers have been teaching, you are a creator, either consciously or unconsciously co-creating your life from the inside out. The universe is run on energy, or *prana*. When you become energetically balanced within yourself, you become capable of miraculous shifts and rearrangements. Visualization is not positive thinking; it is the active focus of harnessing your attention toward who you want to be, what you want to experience – and your soul circle.

CHAPTER 8:

Let Go of the Peanuts

"Everyone is born a genius, but the process of living de-geniuses them."

—Buckminster Fuller

In India, there is a story about how to catch a monkey. You grab a jar or a vase with a thin neck and place peanuts in the bottom of it. The monkey comes along and reaches his hand into the vase to grab the peanuts. His hand becomes a fist that is holding the peanuts, but then he can't get his hand back out of the jar. He has to decide to either keep the peanuts in his hand and remain trapped or let go of the peanuts and be free.

The instinct for self-preservation is built into every living creature on the planet. Even the world's greatest spiritual teachers and thought leaders experience fear. Since you can't avoid fear, you must learn to face it, walk through it, grow from it, and develop your capacity to trust in something bigger than your comfort zone.

The quote by Buckminster Fuller at the top of this chapter states that you are "born a genius." You're born feeling connected to your inner joy. You have faith that you'll be cared for. But, as Mr. Fuller goes on to write, "the process of life de-geniuses you." As you grow up, you begin to identify more with your limiting thoughts and beliefs and become less aware of your inner confidence, freedom, wisdom, and joy. This creates more fear. As you lose sight of who you truly are and the special gifts you possess, you begin to find safety in striving to be like everyone else. Your inner genius – your soul circle – gets overshadowed by anxieties and the fear of not being good enough or having what you need to survive or thrive. You grip anxiety, just as the monkey holds onto the peanuts.

Velcro and Teflon

"Your brain evolved a negativity bias that makes it like Velcro for negative experiences and Teflon for positive ones," said neuroscientist Dr. Rick Hanson. In other words, your brain has a built-in negativity bias, which causes you to remember negative events and focus on the possibility of bad things happening in the future. This bias is part of your brains' effort to protect you from future encounters that resemble the memory of the pain already endured. Conversely, positive events are forgotten easily, not because you don't appreciate them but because they are safe and non-threatening.

Here is a personal example of how one simple negative experience can activate this bias. I have freckles over my nose, chest, shoulders, arms, and legs. When I was about twelve years old, one of my aunts' friends told me that freckles were God's mistake. I have no idea why she would say such a thing. But I do know I spent the next eighteen years trying to cover them up. It didn't matter how many people told me they liked my freckles; what stuck in my brain was the comment that insinuated something was wrong with me. Fear is a powerful force, and so is our negativity bias.

In addition to your negativity bias, you also have a confirmation bias, which causes your brain to take in new information as confirmation of your existing beliefs. This is why no matter how much evidence came into my life that freckles were actually "angel kisses," I only heard it as confirmation of what I already believed, which was that they were God's mistake. If you tend to be anxious, you will find a reason to stay anxious even if new evidence to the contrary is revealed. This is why commitment to a consistent spiritual practice is so vital. You will come to understand that when you are in a state of anxiety or fear, most of your thoughts are not accurate or true.

Internal and External Triggers

Fear runs deep in your physiology. There are two ways fear arises. Fear is either stimulated by external factors such

93

as a real threat or danger in your external environment, or by internal factors such as your thoughts, perceptions, imagination, and projections.

When you are in actual danger, your sympathetic nervous system revs up, and stress hormones are sent throughout your body, preparing you to either fight or take flight. You'll experience this response as an increased heart rate, sweaty palms, or shallow and rapid breathing. Involuntary bodily functions like elimination of waste, digestion, immunity, healing, and sleep get dialed down as your body preserves all of its energy to run. Your mind becomes hyper-focused on the thing that is threatening your safety and how you can escape. This automatic response is incredibly helpful and necessary when you are in real danger.

But when the threat is internal, and this vital life-preserving fear response isn't actually needed, your fight-or-flight response kicks into gear anyway. However, instead of getting activated by external factors, the threat is coming from your mind. The fear arises from your memory, perceptions, and imagination. The human brain isn't able to distinguish the difference between something real or imagined.

Either way it is activated, fear forces you into automatic reactions. You become primal. The fight-or-flight response limits your ability to discern, choose, and respond. Chronic anxiety essentially keeps your brain locked in a limited perception of life, making it unable to see new possibilities and recover from anxiety.

The Buddha teaches, "You are shaped by your thoughts; you become what you think. When your mind is pure, joy follows like a shadow that never leaves. There is nothing so disobedient as an undisciplined mind, and there is nothing so obedient as a disciplined mind."

With a simple daily, breath-centered, mindfulness meditation practice, you can learn how to discipline, and direct, your focus. Sit quietly and close your eyes. Breathe in and out through your nose. Focus your attention on the breath coming in and out of your nostrils. When you feel centered, inhale through your nose, hold your breath at the top of the inhalation, then, exhale, and at the end of your exhalation, mentally, count one. Continue breathing, and counting at the end of every exhale, until you get to ten. Then, start counting backward, counting at the end of every exhale, until you reach one. Do this daily, as a regular meditation practice, or anytime you feel anxious. Through meditation, you can clean your belief window, train your attention, connect to your inner joy, and awaken your power to choose. For this reason, daily meditation is essential, not optional.

Emotional Memory

Anxiety is a habit of both your psychology and your physiology. Your negative thought patterns produce chemicals, which manifest as negative emotions, in your body. Those chemicals, and emotions, signal for your mind to produce more negative thoughts, which produce more negative emotions, like anxiety, and so on. You are projecting out and reflecting back through your awareness of what you already believe. This is your belief window in action. Another way to think about this is that an apple seed can only produce an apple tree. You'll never get an orange tree unless you plant an orange seed. What you believe, feel, and focus on can only produce the likes of themselves. Therefore, you can't create a new reality with the same mental and emotional habits or memories.

When I was young, both of my parents drove while intoxicated while I was in the car. The fear I experienced was profound. I'd get so scared I'd yell and scream, and, when that didn't work, I'd lay down in the seat and close my eyes.

As an adult, sitting in the car while my husband drives, I can sit back and relax. I know I am safe. But sometimes when a car gets too close or someone cuts in front of us, my fight-or-flight response can still kick in. My body remembers the fear I felt as a child in the car with my parents and mistakes it for the new moment I am in, even though I am safe. In yoga, we call this a *vasana*, or "to dwell" or "to remain." Science calls this a neural pathway. You might refer to it, as a trigger.

In this example, the emotional memory of my childhood trauma caused my body to perceive that moment as if I were back in the car with my parents. Signals were sent from my body to my brain, which caused my brain to produce thoughts such as "I've got to get out of this car" or "My husband is reckless." Then, those same thoughts sent signals back to my body to create more of the same fear response, and repeated back and forth. More anxiety only produces more anxiety. When you experience anxiety or stress, chronic or regular states of fight-or-flight respectively, your body holds tighter to past memories, and the habit persists. Your body becomes like your second brain. This type of anxiety or post-traumatic-stress is not actually about the past or the future. It is the result of a body and mind that continues to organize itself, and behave, as if the past or future experience is happening right now.

One way to change this pattern is to consciously stimulate your relaxation response - which is a deep state of inner ease that changes your physical and emotional response to stress - then turn your attention toward a new creation, again and again. As you plant your new seeds of thoughts, emotions, and responses, you must also recognize, that you are both the seed and the gardener.

Your Chosen Truth versus Your Habit

In terms of changing this pattern – no matter why the pattern was created in the first place – you are the only one who can change it. This was hard for me to accept at the beginning of my journey. I wanted to blame. I wanted to stare at the cause and continue to say life was unfair, but that only kept me in more of a state of fight-or-flight. Freedom requires personal responsibility, and that can be the hardest part.

Your belief window is a muscle you can influence. You can develop a chosen truth rather than be driven by your habitual patterns. But your spiritual practice can't just be used for crisis control. Through your daily practice, you become renewed by the clarity of your soul circle, and you also create distance between the part of you that can choose a new response and your habitual thoughts and emotions. However, if you never create distance from your patterns, it's easy to keep confusing your old habits for who you are, which will prolong your suffering.

The ancient wisdom of *The Yoga Sutra* says that when your body holds onto adverse memories, and your mind is left to run wild with anxiety for a prolonged period, you will experience mental and emotional symptoms of dis-ease such as general unhappiness, lack of inner peace, diminished confidence, pessimism, more anxiety, and overall restlessness.

Suffering is always the effect of wrong thought. It is an indication that you are out of harmony with yourself – with the joy and wisdom of your soul circle. The only use of suffering is to help you surrender what is no longer needed, and to reorient your life toward the joy of your being.

Master Your Capacity to Live in a State of Trust

There is only one of two states in which you can live: fear or trust. You are either living in harmony, with your true self, or out of harmony. You cannot live in them both at the same time. This exercise will help you reflect on and identify which state you are in at any given moment.

Draw a vertical line down the middle of a piece of paper so that you have two sections. Title the section on the left "fear" and the section on the right "trust."

> ▷ Fear: In this section, write down all the ways that fear or anxiety manifests for you. Examples: distraction, sleeplessness, digestive issues, procrastination, negative thinking, negative emotions, inability to take deep breaths, physical discomfort, rumination, worry, anger, frustration, nervousness, indecisiveness, feeling overwhelmed, and avoidance.

> ▷ Trust: In this section, write down all the ways trust manifests for you. Examples: feeling present, peaceful, flexible, creative, joyful, safe, decisive, courageous, energized, resilient, excited, hopeful, confident, loving, patient, focused, worthy, happy, and content.

By listing these qualities, you now have more awareness of how you think, feel, and behave when you are in a state of fear, or a state of trust. Remember, when you're in a state of fear you become a prisoner to your anxious habits. However, when you're in a state of trust you will see life from a broader vantage point with more possibilities.

When you choose not to give into your suffering, you can then, choose to use it to remember who you truly are. From this place of power, you can make a new choice about how you will think, believe, feel, and act in your life. Take breaks throughout your day and check-in with which state you are in. Awareness is a vital factor in any change process and in empowering yourself to consciously choose thoughts and emotions that help you stay in harmony with your soul circle.

When you find yourself in a variation of fear, practice this ABC process. This reflection will help you develop greater confidence in your ability to take control of your mental and emotional energy and to master your capacity to live in a state of trust. As you begin to live more in a state of trust, you'll find you are living in the realm of creative energy. You'll also discover you are led more often by your soul circle and therefore are able to choose your way.

The ABCs of Conscious Living

▷ A is for Awareness: Identify and then name the fear or anxiety. For help, use your list from the fear category. Call it what it is. State it as, "I am experiencing [blank]," rather than, "I am [blank]." Notice your dominant thoughts and any emotions that are present. Remember, thoughts produce emotions, and emotions drive your behavior. This is your belief window in action. Pay attention to any sensations in your body. This immediately brings your attention into the moment. Remember that most of your thoughts arising from the fear response are not accurate; they are part of your negativity bias and survival instinct. Your brain is designed to keep you safe, not necessarily happy. Which is another reason awareness is so important.

▷ B is for Breath: Take a minimum of three deep breaths. Breathe in until your belly completely expands. Exhale slowly and smoothly through your nose. Continue breathing like this until you feel your mind settling and your body relaxing. Just by taking these simple breaths you are activating your relaxation response and increasing your capacity to live in a state of trust, and respond in a new way.

▷ C is for Choose: Choose a quality from your trust list. Within every experience, there is a contrast. By naming what you are feeling from the fear category – what you don't want –you can choose its opposite from your trust list – what you do want. Then, embody the quality, similarly as you would in the visualization practice from Chapter 7. Release your jaw and shoulders and relax your stomach. Continue this process until you experience a positive shift, or feel in greater harmony with your true self.

Liberation comes from knowing your true nature, not just knowing about it. Experiencing positive shifts in your mind, body, and soul requires you to slow down and become present to your life, to your emotional states, and to your soul circle. You must participate in cultivating the inner conditions during which you can thrive. Trust leads to more happiness and harmony, and happiness is scientifically correlated with increased well-being, and more confidence and joy.

CHAPTER 9:

Set Yourself Free

*"Darkness cannot drive out darkness; only light
can do that. Hate cannot drive out hate; only
love can do that."*

—Martin Luther King, Jr.

Your Limitless Potential for Happiness, Freedom, and Joy

Forgiveness is a spiritual principle that receives the most resistance because it is often the most misunderstood. Your ego, which is on your belief window, isn't concerned with your happiness or freedom; it just wants to be right. The need to be right is the mindset of a victim. It leaves you helpless and dependent on too many factors that are simply out of your control. The best gift you can give yourself and the world is your happiness and joy.

If you knew your potential to feel truly happy, joyous, and free, you would release yourself from the impossible desire to control the world, your partner, or your child.

You would realize that you are the one who creates your reality, not them.

Expecting my childhood to be any different than it was just kept me trapped. I was in a constant mental and emotional battle with a past I couldn't possibly change. I was stuck. Forgiveness is a decision you make because it sets you free. When you forgive, you win. This is one of the hardest spiritual truths to internalize and practice because your mind wants to hold onto blame for as long as it can. But that only increases anxiety and separates you from your soul circle, which is the source of your joy.

If you are suffering and you want to suffer less, you must become willing to let go and ultimately forgive. Places within you that are blocked by fear will become liberated. You will open yourself up to unshakable spiritual confidence and freedom.

Turning Your Resentments Upside Down

When I first began my spiritual journey, I was asked to take an inventory of my resentments and grudges. The list was long. It included both of my grandmothers, my stepdad, the men who harmed me, my aunt, the people at the bar where my mom worked who always lied to me, the boy I thought was supposed to save me, and especially my mom and dad.

As I made this list, I remember thinking, "I'll never forgive my mom and dad." I was sure of that. I was just as certain my mentor was going to agree with me. I knew that after she heard my story, she would see things from my perspective, side with me, and understand why it would be impossible for me to forgive my parents. We met, and she listened for hours as I shared my story. She was patient, kind, and compassionate. She agreed that I had lived through a painful childhood and that the actions of the adults in my life had been wrong.

Then she asked me to do something that made my head spin. She wanted me to reflect on how my unwillingness to forgive my parents affected my choices and behaviors, as well as my happiness. She wanted me to reflect on myself, not my parents. I was confused. Had I not made it clear they were the problem, not me? I resisted. She gently reminded me that our work together was about examining my life, not theirs. She wasn't asking me to forgive my parents, just to reflect on how not forgiving them was hurting me or causing me to consciously or unconsciously harm others. This was not easy because I was in the habit of seeing myself as the victim. I was focused on how my life had been ruined because of their choices and my awful childhood. Now I was being asked to look at myself. I was in unfamiliar territory.

The process she invited me into is rooted in two powerful spiritual actions called *tapas* and *svadhyaya*. Tapas is the action of refining your mental habits – and cleaning your belief window – by doing something different. A new behavior, such as the one my mentor had asked me to do, often produces friction or tension because it goes against the grain of your habits. *Svadhyaya* is the practice of studying the resistance, insights, or feedback created by your new behavior.

For example, as I examined my life from this new perspective, I noticed how often I would blame my parents or point to the past as the reasons why I couldn't succeed or be happy. Another reflection that came from this practice was when I noticed I had a lot of jealousy toward my roommate. She easily expressed her needs and had no problem asking for what she wanted. I, however, had a long-held belief, accumulated from childhood, that it was not okay to want things and, it was never ever okay to rely on other people. So, I resented her. It became clear that my inability to forgive my parents caused me to put up walls between other people and me, to create limitations in my life, to diminish my ability to be happy, and to justify my poor choices. Harboring resentment was also keeping me stuck in fear and unable to be vulnerable or forgive myself and others.

There Is a Reason Why Every Spiritual Tradition Emphasizes Forgiveness

The more I committed to nurturing my happiness and peace of mind, the more it became clear I couldn't hold onto those feelings and be free. Not only does every spiritual tradition emphasize the practice of forgiveness, but modern science and recent studies indicate that negative states of mind and negative emotions affect your self-worth, health, and overall success in life. They can even negatively change the expression of your DNA. Your unwillingness to forgive is like torturing yourself and expecting the other person to feel the pain.

Your spiritual practice is aimed at cleaning and refining your belief window. You can't clean anyone else's window. When you cling to resentment, blame, and anger, it's hard to feel and experience your worthiness. Forgiveness is not forgetting. Forgiveness doesn't mean the absence of boundaries. It is not accepting hurtful behavior or denying something was painful. You don't even have to ever tell the other person you have forgiven them. It is the process of withdrawing your attention from the thing that is keeping you out of your soul circle.

Whether you forgive someone or not doesn't change them; it changes you. Forgiveness is a byproduct of doing inner work and weeding out the triggers embedded in your mind, body, and heart. It is an outcome of daily surrenders, or what, in yoga, is called *isvarapranidhana*.

After my dad was released from the hospital, I asked him to tell me his life story. I sat silently for two hours just listening to him talk about his life. I'd already been working on forgiving my dad, but hearing his life experience freed me even more. Forgiveness can be so much more than letting go of the pain and the blocks that keep us from being happy. It can become an opportunity for spiritual wisdom and radical insights into love and our true nature. My dad spent his life searching for happiness. He told me he had to work hard every day to feel okay, just like I had.

Last Christmas, my mom and I were wrapping presents for my son. As we wrapped, I thought about my childhood and how I don't have great memories of the holidays. Then I asked my mom about her Christmases as a child. She told me there were many Christmases when she didn't receive any presents at all. My mom lived in a house with holes in the walls and an outhouse in the backyard for a bathroom. Life is complex. It is not one-sided. It is multi-dimensional. My mom was not able to be the mom she would have liked to have been for me. She has expressed her regret and sadness. We can't go back and change the past, but we can go forward from where we are. Through forgiveness, many of my anxieties and fears have been dusted off my belief window. I can see that she also is human and has come a long way. Things may not have been the way I would have liked as a child, but from where she came, she did all she was capable of doing for me, and her life today is quite a success story.

The cause of another person's actions, choices, or words has nothing to do with you. Every pain and harm in the world is rooted in fear. If we were all connected to our soul circle, and our belief windows were clean and free of fears, attachments, and aversions, there would be a lot less suffering in the world. Life would still include obstacles and opportunities, but you wouldn't have to take it all so personally. You'd be driven by love rather than your expectations about how things have to be in order to feel happy. It's crucial to internalize that joy is your true nature, not suffering. It's necessary to know that life changes when you change.

During the last visit I had with my dad before he died, we shared long talks about love and forgiveness. He knew I forgave him, and I knew he loved me, but he still had trouble forgiving himself. I made him a little affirmation card that said, "I forgive myself, and I release all shame and guilt." He would say it again and again as he rested in bed, barely able to breathe. I would say it with him and for him when he couldn't.

Forgiveness Is the Attribute of the Strong

Love is power. Mahatma Gandhi, whose entire mission in India was based on non-violence and non-harming, said, "The weak can never forgive. Forgiveness is the attribute of the strong." Forgiveness breeds peace. Resentment breeds suffering. Jesus cured the sick and dying with love. He forgave everyone for everything because he could separate the choices people made out of fear from the essential nature of their soul. He said you too can do what I do. When we love ourselves enough to forgive, we heal.

One of the most loving things a mentor ever did for me was tell me she couldn't help me. I was being particularly stubborn about a resentment I had toward someone who harmed me. We both agreed their behavior was inappropriate, but I was unwilling to see it from any other perspective. She told me if I wanted to be free, I'd have to change my story. She didn't judge me for my "stuck-ness," but she also wasn't going to agree with the story I had created about "poor me." In the end, no amount of support or awareness will change you if you are unwilling to change yourself. No one else can think for you; no one else can narrate your life for you. It is up to you.

Catherine Ponder, the author of many new-thought books, wrote, "The world you live in is the exact record of your thoughts. If you do not like the world you live in, then you do not like your thoughts. An uplifted mind is a magnet for all good things of the universe to hasten to you. Whereas, a depressed, anxious, critical, or resentful mind becomes a magnet for trouble to fly to you. The choice is up to you." This has nothing to do with what you deserve or are worthy of. It is about what you allow or resist to be on your belief window.

Sometimes things happen, and we may never understand why. Other times, things we want so badly just don't manifest. In my positive psychology program, my teacher Tal Ben-Shahar said, "Not everything happens for the best, but some people make the best of everything that happens."

Research conducted by Diener & Seligman studied happy people versus unhappy people. One vital difference found between the two groups was their interpretation style. Both groups confirmed they experienced sadness, setbacks, disappointments, heartbreak, and loss. The difference between their happiness and unhappiness was in their perception. Happy people discern the circumstances or events in their life as temporary, isolated, and part of being human. Unhappy people view these events as permanent, pervasive, and personal. This is called learned helplessness and can lead to anxiety and a sense of disempowerment and even depression.

As I was growing up, nothing in life seemed fair. My childhood didn't have happy traditions or summer vacations and picnics. I felt alone and isolated most of the time. But I have learned that if I want to experience my life today differently, then I have to be different. Even though life is not always simple or fair, you are always free to choose how you respond and the meaning you make out of anything and everything.

Four Levels of Forgiveness

The Yoga Sutra teaches that when your mind is disturbed by negative thought patterns, you should cultivate the opposite pattern through the practice of *pratipaksha bhavana*, or cultivating the opposite viewpoint. It is suggested you replace anger with compassion, violent thoughts with peaceful ones, hate with love, and even replace your anxiety with a sense of contentment.

Looking at forgiveness through these four levels will give you a path to heal your wounds and surrender negative states of mind and emotional blocks that only hold you back from truly reclaiming your inner joy. You do not have to start at level one, and you may find you never get to level four with certain people, but the key is to practice and to do what you can. Start from where you are and stay willing to forgive yourself and others.

▷ Take Responsibility: Release blame and take ownership of the life you want to live today. Examine how not forgiving hurts you and possibly causes you to justify your poor choices in life, including limiting beliefs and where you feel stuck.

▷ See from The Other Person's Perspective: This isn't about right or wrong. This is simply about seeing it from their viewpoint. Put yourself in their shoes. Learn more about them as I did with my mom and dad. Consider their life story and why they might have done what they did or didn't do.

▷ Become Willing to Create a New Viewpoint: I used to focus on how much I missed out on as a child because of my parent's alcoholism and neglect. But now I can also say that as a child, I learned to be more sensitive and empathetic to others. Because of what I went through, I can help so many more people today, and I know my power and capacity for joy.

▷ Say Thank You for the Experience: This is a deep level of spiritual practice. Saying thank you to the experience is not about approving or condoning hurtful behavior from yourself or others. It requires turning your attention away from the other person and toward your soul circle. Forgiveness at this level means you have found a way to integrate the hurt, or difficult experience into your life by extracting the wisdom you can gain from having gone through it, even as you let people or conditions go away. This is where you ask yourself, "What is the spiritual lesson in this for me?" or "How can having faced this allow me to also help others?" Then, you surrender and release the residue of what you no longer need to carry. You set yourself free.

When you release resistance and forgive, you are restored to soundness of mind. I believe this is what Pema Chodron meant when she wrote about allowing our circumstances to soften us and make us kinder. Rather than reliving what you cannot change, try changing what you can change. You can change your response, your choices, and your perspective. You can choose to forgive and set yourself free.

CHAPTER 10:

Choose Your Reality

---

*"We are what we repeatedly do. Excellence, then,
is not an act, but a habit."*

—Aristotle

When You Change, Everything Changes

We were sitting in a huge arena with thousands of people when I leaned toward my husband and said, "I am not walking on fire." We were attending a Tony Robbins event called "Unleash the Power Within," which I'd heard concluded with a fire walk. I had no idea what to expect, but I was certain I was not going to walk on fire. Five days later – you guessed it – I walked on fire.

Throughout this book, I've shared personal stories about my life. I've shared them because I want you to know, deep in your being, that change is possible. I want you to know with complete certainty that you can face your fears, solve your anxiety, and become greater than you were before.

There was a time in my life when I couldn't walk into a room of strangers without twitching and frantically looking around for a place where I could hide and not be noticed. Today, I can stand in front of hundreds of people and speak. I can write this book and tell you some of my darkest secrets, which, for years, I believed made me unworthy and broken. I can do this because those limiting beliefs and fears no longer define me. They are no longer my story. They are not my chosen reality. Instead, I have reconnected to my soul circle and feel truly comfortable in my skin. I have internalized the spiritual truth that the way I experience my life – what I think, believe, feel, and choose – is happening from me, not to me.

During the event, Tony Robbins said, "We all have the power to change our lives. But most people don't have the discipline to control their mental focus." His words echoed the teaching in *The Yoga Sutra*, which, in part, defines yoga as the practice of having complete mastery over the fluctuations of your mind. In today's modern Western yoga system, there is little mental discipline. People don't tend to practice sitting still for long. They want to change their mindset but are unwilling to change their mental habits.

Habits are not mysterious. As long as your emotional and mental home base is anxiety, it doesn't matter what happens, good or bad; you will find your way back to your habit.

116

Yoga says that whatever you bind your mind to is what you will become. Your future is influenced by the choices you make right now. When *you* change, everything around you changes. When you stay the same, everything seems to stay the same. You can change your reality and transform your life based on what you choose to dedicate your mind, emotions, and heart to. This is what, in yoga, is called *sankalpa*, or intention. It is the practice of harnessing your will to change the course of your life. A *sankalpa* in scientific context is a form of neuroplasticity, which is the ability of your brain to change how you process yourself and the world in a specific way based on what you consciously or unconsciously choose.

Make the Unconscious Conscious

My husband grew up on a small dairy farm in Washington State near the Canadian border. No one ever told him he couldn't strive for dreams bigger than what his small town could provide, but no one also ever told him he could. He unconsciously made the assumption that he couldn't. It was his limiting beliefs and lack of knowledge about what was possible for him that held him back for years. He spent more than a decade doing electrical work, which he despised, and, as a result, his focus grew further away from his soul circle. He became disconnected from his truth. He had what he thought was an impossible dream, and it was eating him alive inside. He desperately wanted to leave that little town to study and play music.

In his early thirties, he finally did. He moved to Seattle and eventually to Los Angeles where he earned his music degree. Another decade later, we now live in Nashville, where he spends much of his days songwriting. But all that wasn't a possibility for him until he changed the way he saw himself and his options and committed to new ways of thinking, believing, feeling, and acting, even when it was hard. He faced his fears, walked through uncertainty, and became willing to trade in the pain of staying the same for the discomfort of growth. As he did, it literally changed his psychology, physiology, and biology – and, therefore, his reality.

To change your story, you must learn to acknowledge your past and your fears without letting them control or limit what you do now. Trying to avoid pain will not get you the outcome of joy, confidence, and inner trust. Resistance will only deepen your habit of anxiety. Knowing you want to feel less anxious is not the same thing as declaring and affirming your happiness, freedom, and joy.

Donuts and Happiness

In my workshops, I often ask participants to draw a donut. Ninety-nine percent of people draw a large circle with a small circle inside of it. When I ask the same room of people to draw happiness, every single person draws a different picture. That's because, unlike the image of a donut, happiness isn't a universal picture. It varies for each of us. You must define it, choose it, live it, and sustain it. You must become it.

When parents are asked what they want most for their children, they answer health, happiness, joy, love, success, confidence, and good relationships – a meaningful life. Now consider what you learned in school: math, history, spelling, reading, and so on. While those are important subjects, so is fulfillment. Happiness, joy, confidence, and love aren't subjects you're taught in school, and yet they're qualities and experiences we all seek.

Your Object of Focus

Samadhi is a Sanskrit word that means complete absorption with your object of focus. Traditionally, in yoga psychology, it means total union with your true nature – your soul circle. At the deepest levels of samadhi, your attention is so linked with your object of focus that you are no longer aware of any separation. Essentially, you become your object of focus.

This may sound so esoteric you can't relate it to your life here and now. But the truth is you experience a form of *samadhi* every moment of every day. You are often so linked with your thoughts – and your anxious thoughts – that you essentially become the thought. You can't distinguish between the part of you observing the thought (your soul circle), the thought itself (your belief window), and the reality you're experiencing (the world circle – what is being reflected back to you).

What you believe, you perceive. What you put your faith into, you expect. Your focus is truly a superpower; it is creative energy. Ask yourself, is what you regularly pay attention to bringing you more sustained joy or not? If what you focus on produces more anxiety and doesn't bring you closer to your true nature of confidence, wisdom, and joy, you need to change your object of focus.

To Become Familiar With

One of the definitions of the word meditation is "to become familiar with." You may think of meditation as only something you do with your eyes closed while sitting on a cushion or in a chair, but meditation is also the process of becoming familiar with your chosen reality. It is becoming absorbed moment-to-moment in daily life with the thoughts, beliefs, feelings, and choices that bring you into alignment with who you want to be, how you want to live, and who you truly are.

The process of any meditation begins with your ability to focus your attention to one point, what, in yoga, is called *dharana*. Most people mistake the practice of trying to focus their attention as meditation itself, but really it is a preparatory practice. For example, if you want to feel less anxious and more confident, you first have to practice gathering your attention away from the anxious thoughts and focusing your attention on thoughts that make you feel more strong and stable. But at first, you won't necessarily feel more strong and stable. At this beginning stage, you are simply putting your effort into the action of bringing your wandering mind back again and again.

Once you can hold your attention to one point, the next stage of meditation is to keep it there for an extended period of time, what, in yoga, is called, *dhyana*. This is what leads to *samadhi,* or complete absorption with your chosen point of focus. For example, your anxious thoughts feel so real because you have mastered your ability to focus and sustain your attention on them.

A Spiritual Formula

You can use this same spiritual formula to free yourself from anxiety. With commitment and consistency, you can develop *samadhi* and become linked with your chosen reality. When I began working with my teacher in Los Angeles, one of the first assignments he gave me was to clarify my values. He said that to change my mind from negative to positive and from scattered to confident, I'd have to first get clear on my core values. I had to make decisions and discernments about what I wanted to experience in life and who I wanted to become. In other words, I had to choose a new reality before I could become absorbed in it.

Facing Your Unconscious Façade

On a piece of paper, draw a small circle. Draw another small circle around that small circle. Draw a large circle around the two circles.

The small circle in the center represents your core values. Deep within you are all of your dreams, gifts, passions, desires, and everything that makes you uniquely you. It is the you underneath all the residue on your belief window. The part of you, that your soul circle, wants to help you experience, what, in yoga, is called, your *dharma*, or purpose.

The middle circle represents all of your fears, limiting beliefs, and anxieties. This middle circle becomes the wall that blocks you from experiencing your true nature and becoming established in who you truly want to be.

The most outer circle represents your façade or protective layer. You created this façade to hide your fears and limiting beliefs from other people and the world around you. For example, my fear of not being good enough caused me to create the façade that I was super independent, always perky, and problem-free.

Your façade becomes another layer blocking you off from your soul circle, and your core values. This blockage from who you truly are creates more anxiety and fear and sometimes causes you to put up more walls, which only cuts you off further from your core values and from true happiness and joy.

My client, Sean, was extremely successful in his career, but he was also unhappy. Afraid he'd let his family and colleagues down if he left, he continued to move up the corporate ladder of success for more than two decades. He endured years of anxiety, feeling overwhelmed, insomnia, and overall life dissatisfaction. Through our work together, Sean faced his fears, shed his façade, and reconnected to his soul circle and his core values. He consciously chose his new reality and owned his gifts, dreams, and desires. Sean finally left his career and carved a new path for his life, one that is driven by *his* truth and that makes him happy.

I encourage you to go back to Chapter 4 and review the fears and limiting beliefs you wrote about in terms of your belief window. Then, to identify your façade or the image you've created to hide your fears from the world, answer the following questions. Your answers will also help you discover how your fears, limiting beliefs, and façade are blocking you from who you truly want to be.

▷ What image or façade do you present to the world? Consider all the areas of your life, such as friends, community, family, and work. You may have developed a unique façade for different areas of your life.

▷ Now give your façade one name. Naming it will help you distance your identity from it because you are perceiving it now, rather than being it.

▷ How do you act when your façade is present?

123

▷ How do you feel when your façade is present?

▷ What is your façade protecting you from?

▷ How long has your façade been with you?

▷ Who is your façade keeping you from becoming, or being, more of in your life?

▷ Who would you be if this façade were gone?

▷ What do you want or need to say to your façade to let the image go?

Inner Engineering a Chosen Identity

Sometimes it's hard to see your own strengths. You are often so focused on what you don't want that you can't articulate exactly what you do want. This journaling practice will help you get that clear.

Write about three people you admire, and what you admire most about each of them. These can be people you know, people from history, fictional characters, or world leaders. Write a separate description for each person. Write as if you were going to introduce this person to your friends and family. Include all of the positive attributes and character traits you love about them. Take your time with this. Get it all down on paper.

When you're finished, review the three stories you wrote. Put a circle around all of the positive character traits and attributes you can find about each person in each story.

Then, on a separate piece of paper, write down all of the positive traits from your three stories until you have one long list of positive attributes and character traits. Write each attribute in the following format: she/he is, she/he does, or she/he has. For example, instead of just writing "confident," write "she is confident," or "she is true to herself," or "he is courageous," or "he is open to what is possible."

Next, on a new piece of paper, write about a time when you were at your best. Think about a time when you felt like you were truly in the flow – when you were happy, free, and truly you. This can be a period in your life, an event, or even a moment. Write about this time when you were at your best in the same way you did when you wrote about the people you admired.

Then, circle all the positive traits you can find in your story and add them to the long list of attributes you created earlier. Write your character traits in the following format: "I am fearless" or "I am at ease with myself."

Next, look over the long list of positive attributes you now have. This list will be a combination of traits from your story and the stories you wrote about the three people you admire.

Now, choose and circle four to eight character traits from your long list that represent who you truly want to become more of in your life. Choose attributes that resonate with your core values. These may not be attributes you currently own right now, but they are ones that you are ready to commit to nurturing, practicing, and becoming that will bring you closer to embodying your true self.

Finally, on a separate piece of paper, write down the four to eight character traits you circled, in this format: "I am..." and complete the sentence. For example, "I am optimistic," or "I am powerful," or "I feel strong," or "I have the power to become whoever I want to be."

One of the most important steps in any spiritual or yoga practice is to clarify your values, which are your chosen realities and truths. If you don't decide who you want to be, everyone else will decide how you should show up in your life and what you should focus on for you, and the pattern of anxiety will persist. Without a vision, you will constantly be pulled by your past and your habits.

Your "I Am" Statements

The "I am..." statements you created are more powerful than any other affirmations you'll ever read, recite, or practice because they are rooted in your core values and your chosen reality.

Affirmations are statements you repeat with emotion and intention. In other words, you don't just say them and hope they work. You must aim to believe in them. When affirmations are practiced in an effective way – with emotion and followed with action – they become new neural pathways wired into your nervous system that can override old habits of anxiety, fear, and self-doubt, what, in yoga, is called, *samskara*. You literally become established in your core values, and your soul circle. Your new affirmations are qualities you have chosen to "firm up" in your mental, emotional, and physical life and become *absorbed* with. In yoga, these statements are referred to as *mantras* – *ma* meaning mind and *tra* meaning traverse – because they help you traverse anxiety, fear, and the mental façade you've created. They also act as potent seeds for new perspectives, possibilities, and ideas that get planted into your powerful subconscious when done with extended focus.

The next step is to put them into action. Take time each morning to tune into these guiding mantras.

▷ Every day, week, or month, choose one or two mantras from your list to focus on and become absorbed with.

▷ In the morning, journal about the affirmations you have chosen. As you consider your day, think about how you can embody these new values so that you can live more aligned with your who you want to be and the reality you want to experience. For example, if you chose the value, "I am confident," write about what that looks like in your actual life. How will you walk, talk, sit, think, feel, and breathe differently than your protective façade may have? How will you greet people? How will you meet challenges when they arise? Get as specific as you can in your journaling.

▷ Next, close your eyes and visualize what you just wrote about. Remember, visualization is not just wishful or positive thinking; it is the harnessing of your energy and focus. It is the mental and emotional equivalent of seeing, feeling, and becoming on the inside what you want to create on the outside. This is *samadhi*. When your mind wanders, repeat your affirmation silently or out loud. Stay in your visualization until it feels complete.

▷ Then, put your new values into action throughout your day. Prime your environment with reminders.

An old Cherokee grandfather told his grandson a story. "A fight is going on inside me," he said. "It is a terrible fight between two wolves. One is evil; he is anger, envy, greed, arrogance, resentment, and self-pity." He continued, "The other is good; he is joy, peace, love, hope, serenity, humility, kindness, empathy, generosity, truth, compassion, and faith. This same fight is going on inside of you, Grandson, and inside of every other person on the planet." The grandson pondered this for a moment and then asked, "Grandfather, which wolf will win?" The old man smiled and simply said, "The one you feed."

The more you visualize, embody, and behave in your life as your chosen self, the more your chosen reality will become your default. Making your ideal real on the inside will help you to overcome negative thinking and clear away fear, limiting beliefs, and other debris from your belief window. As you repeat, visualize, and act out your core values, you are literally rewiring your reticular activating system, the evidence finding filter in your brain, to find evidence to prove your new chosen reality right.

Repetition is key. It's how you master any new habit. Anxiety is a mental, emotional, and physical habit. But so is confidence, trust, and joy. Which habit will you feed?

CHAPTER 11:

The Obstacles You'll Encounter

"It is rare or almost impossible that an event can be negative from all points of view."
—The Dalai Lama

At the beginning of this book, I shared that the spiritual life is experiential, not academic. I wrote that the problem with anxiety is that it never was your problem and that your spiritual practice is not designed to fix you because you're not broken. I emphasized it would be your readiness to these principles that would transform your life, not just learning about them. Your new path – to reclaim your joy – requires your attention, consistency, and commitment, because old habits, such as anxiety, run deep. You will not experience the joy that is yours to reclaim if you give all of your energy to symptom relief and never change the patterns that are keeping you from it.

The Yoga Sutra lays out specific obstacles you will surely encounter, such as impatience, regression, lack of focus, inability to commit, lethargy, uncertainty, and self-doubt, which, for the anxious mind, if you are not careful, can become boulders in the way of happiness and clarity. Life will always continue to change, and uncertainty will always be part of your experience. Fear and limiting beliefs will surface. Your impulse will be to push them away or to judge yourself or others. You will have moments when you question your confidence and progress. You'll fall victim to old thoughts, beliefs, and reactions that previously kept you trapped in anxiety. Don't wish for your problems to go away. Instead, reach for a higher perspective, and get back into mental, and emotional harmony, with your true nature. Every challenge can either be a problem or an opportunity depending on how you choose to perceive it.

One of the biggest obstacles you'll face is your belief that you can do this all on your own. Although the answers are already within you, a great mentor, teacher, or coach will help you see what's hiding in your blind spots. One of my early teachers would often say, "You can't see the spinach in your teeth, but I can see it." In other words, a great teacher can help you see an alternate viewpoint even when your mind is stuck on misperceptions, negative thinking, or fear. A teacher can help you remember who you are even on days when you forget.

In Western culture, we celebrate independence, but it is interdependence that helps you thrive. Anxiety and fear left unchanged will reactivate your protective façade and rebuild the walls of limiting beliefs around your freedom and joy. I know for sure I would not be where I am today without my teacher, my spiritual community, and, most importantly, my daily practice.

Transformation is empowering, magical, and messy all at the same time. It's like untangling a large ball of yarn. You pull at one end of the string, and soon the whole thing becomes unraveled. But with that same ball of yarn, you can create something wonderful and beautiful. Your personal internal undoing and rebuilding are similar. It is not a straight line but a complicated ball of string with knots, tangles, and hidden possibilities. The reality of your life is that it will become better when you become better. Embrace and embody the principles laid out in this book. As you do, you will find that you can recreate yourself and finally break free from your struggle with anxiety and self-doubt.

Most importantly, remember every day to reflect on the brilliancy of your own soul. Take time to reconnect to your inner joy because when you do, you are a connecting to who you truly are.

CHAPTER 12:

Follow Your Joy

———

"Find a place inside where there's joy, and the joy will burn out the pain"

—Joseph Campbell

Toward the end of his life, my dad asked me, "How did you get to be you?" His question, touched my heart. He admired who I had become in spite of all that I went through. I would answer by saying the first requirement is that I believed in the possibility of great joy and that I committed every day to be established in it. As my father was recovering from his alcoholism, he would tell me he had to choose every day to be happy, and to live in a state of trust, and harmony. He experienced a lot of pain in his life too, but he made the decision to forgive those who hurt him so he could have peace. In the end, he became one of my greatest teachers. I admired him as much as he admired me. Tears of gratitude fill my eyes now as I write this because all I feel when I think of him is love.

This is just one of the many blessings and benefits I have received through my journey.

This may sound strange after reading what my childhood was like, but I have found that it is through facing your darkest places instead of pushing them away that your soul expands. When you do, you'll find that we are all connected by love, and are essentially one. What you feel toward someone else, you absorb. What you hold in your mental and emotional body becomes part of you. It's making your way through the mess, not staring at it, that you gain access to your inner stability. You will discover that you are the author of your life story, and that is a wonderful thing to truly embrace.

My purpose for writing this book was to share with you that no matter what you face now or have gone through in your past, you are capable of great joy. As the Dalai Lama says, "Happiness is not ready-made. It comes from your own actions." My wish for you is that you feel connected every day to your inner strength and joy – to your soul circle. I want you to know that there is no endpoint to your freedom and happiness once you choose it.

I can say with complete certainty that if you apply the principles in this book, you can experience profound changes in the way you think, believe, feel, and act in your life. You will find yourself reconnecting to who you truly are, and living with confidence and deep inner happiness and joy.

In the first principle, you discovered your belief window. You learned that your mindset is the most influential operating system for your life. How you experience life is, in great part, a reflection of what you already think, believe, and feel. Therefore, if you want to experience life differently, you have to become different on the inside first, and create new beliefs.

In the second principle, you were introduced to the three core misperceptions that perpetuate your anxiety. When you're stuck in negative thinking, misperception, and old patterns, your mind unconsciously recreates the same experience over and over again and moves you further from your soul circle until you finally hit a spiritual bottom. You learned that anxiety is not a problem you must overcome, or a sign of failure. Anxiety is powerful feedback that can help you navigate your life with more mastery.

Then, in the third principle, you were asked to make the most important decision a spiritual seeker can make, which is to take ownership of your life, especially your *inner* life. You learned that, although help is almost always required, no one is coming to do the moment-to-moment work for you. Obstacles and pain are universal aspects of everyone's life. Taking personal responsibility is the only way to integrate your challenges, extract the lessons, and rise above limiting circumstances and beliefs that exaggerate your anxiety for years. Change can be hard, but here you saw how it is always possible.

The fourth principle emphasized the importance of a daily – even sometimes moment-to-moment – practice of focusing your attention on what you do want rather than what you don't want. Yoga psychology defines visualization as the ability to experience your desired outcome with your whole self before it happens in your outer life. The more you can see it and feel it, the closer you are to it. You can rewire your nervous system for new reactions through your capacity to imagine, believe, and create new inner scenarios. This principle is a beautiful combination of focus and detachment.

In the fifth principle, you discovered that there are only two states you can live in: fear or trust. When you live in a state of trust, and harmony with your true nature, you are less reactive and more in control. You raise your creative frequency and activate your power of choice. You live from a higher vantage point with more possibilities.

In the sixth principle, you were introduced to one of the most potent truths for transformation, which is forgiveness. Surrendering resentment and blame takes courage and strength. Forgiveness is a byproduct of doing your inner work. It is by letting go of what you were not meant to hold that you free yourself to reconnect with your spiritual power.

Within the seventh principle, you faced many of your longest-held fears and shed the protective façade you created to hide them from the world around you. You looked deep within and established your core values and the reality you want to live.

As you continue to put these principles into action, you will find yourself deeply established in your true nature. You will determine the direction of your life. You will be present with challenges and uncertainty without attachment and fear. No matter what happens, you will know how to manage and master what goes on within you. You will have an unshakeable relationship with your inner guidance system. You'll experience increasing happiness and freedom. You will be amazed at who you are, what you're capable of, and the joy you have reclaimed.

Become the Safest Place You Know

Close your eyes and bring to mind one of the safest places you've ever been to. This might be the ocean, your home, a grandparent's home, your yoga mat, or a retreat. Wherever it is, see this place as you can in your mind's eye. Allow your body to relax. Soften your heart so you can take in all the sensations as if you are right there, safe and comfortable. Stay there a moment. Breathe it in. Feel it.

Now, imagine that this safe place – the safest place you know – is *you*. As the poet Rumi beautifully wrote, "What you seek is seeking you." What if you didn't allow fear, self-doubt, or anxiety to live inside of you. What if *you* were the safest place you've ever been to? Take that in for a moment. Feel the peace, joy, and safety right there in your own soul circle – within your being.

Acknowledgments

I've spent so much time thinking about this section of my book. I want to honor and acknowledge all of the love, support and guidance that I have received over the last two decades.

I'd like to begin by thanking my husband, Eric. We met almost twenty years ago when I was just beginning my spiritual journey. I was full of anxiety, but with your love, support, and patience, you allowed me the grace, and the time, to untangle from my fears, and self-doubt, without taking any of it personally. You put up a mirror to the joy that is in my own being and helped me learn how to let it shine. The confidence you have in who you are allowed me to be who I am. I love you.

Next, I'd like to thank my mother, Debbie, and my father, Brad. You two have been among my greatest teachers, and without you, I would not be the person I am today. I thank you for doing your best, even when you were scared, and unsure, and without any early role models of your own.

I admire and honor the individuals you became in spite of your own difficult beginnings. I love you both.

To My Personal Teachers

Maureen, thank you for loving me enough to be honest with me, and not giving in to my stories of "poor me." You helped me develop the clarity and courage to change what I can change. Thank you, for sharing with me, your fears and shortcomings, so I could face mine. I love you.

Lynda, you introduced me to books, concepts, and ideas that opened my mind and heart. Your guidance changed the trajectory of my life. You showed me how to trust myself and see beyond my obstacles and limitations. I love you so much.

Robert, thank you for introducing me to a dynamic, profound, and practical way to study *The Yoga Sutra*. You have a gift for making complex teachings, relevant to our modern times. Thank you for showing me how to make them personal for my life. My recovery from anxiety is in great part because of your critical and deep insights about the nature of the mind.

Amy, I can't imagine where I'd be without your guidance. Not only did you write the foreword to this book, which I am deeply humbled by, but you helped me bring *The Yoga Sutra* into my heart. You showed me how to take the teachings from academic to experiential, and make that long journey from information to transformation. I admire you beyond words, and I love you from the bottom of my heart.

Thank you to my friends and family for all of your encouragement and support. Your messages, notes, and cards meant the world to me during this crazy, and wonderful, writing process.

To my writing team at Difference Press, led by Dr. Angela Lauria, thank you for making this book possible. Thank you for creating the space for me to bring this book to life, and share with my readers what is possible when we reconnect to who we truly are.

Thank You

I want to offer you a special thank you for reading my book. If you are a spiritual seeker, who's worked hard on yourself, and you're already armed with tools to manage your anxiety, but you want more than symptom relief, I have a special gift for you. If you want to experience confidence that endures, and joy that truly lasts, let's have a conversation about how you can internalize, embrace and implement the principles in this book. If you want to talk to someone who knows how you feel, and can help, I want to invite you to schedule a free one-hour call with me. To schedule your call, visit my website, www.joystonecoaching.com

About the Author

Joy Stone is a professional speaker, a mindset and spiritual life coach, a best-selling author, and a positive psychology and yoga therapy practitioner who is educated in yoga psychology. Known for her ability to deliver profound spiritual teachings in a practical and modern way, Joy works closely with spiritual seekers who want more than symptom relief for their anxiety, they want to find their center and reclaim their joy. Joy's Soul School Coaching Program blends eastern and western psychology and philosophy, and has helped countless spiritual seekers move from information overload to lasting inner transformation.

With more than two decades of personal anxiety experience, Joy shares her professional experience with the world through workshops, retreats, books, and speaking engagements.

Joy received her positive psychology education at the Whole-Being Institute under Harvard Professor Tal Ben-Shahar, and her yoga teaching certification under the Anusara style – a therapeutic application of yoga philosophy and practice.

Joy lives in Nashville, Tennessee, with her husband, Eric, and son, Jack.

Website: www.joystonecoaching.com

Facebook: https://www.facebook.com/joystonecoaching/

Instagram: https://www.instagram.com/joystonecoaching/

First Meditation

I know that I am pure spirit, that I always have been, and that I always will be. There is inside me a place of confidence and quietness and security where all things are known and understood. This is the Universal Mind, God, of which I am a part and which responds to me as I ask of it.

This Universal Mind knows the answer to all of my problems, and even now the answers are speeding their way to me. I needn't struggle for them; I needn't worry or strive for them. When the time comes, the answers will be there. I give my problems to the great mind of God; I let go of them, confident that the correct answers will return to me when they are needed. Through the great law of attraction, everything in life that I need for my work and fulfillment will come to me. It is not necessary that I strain about this – only believe. For in the strength of my belief, my faith will make it so. I see the hand of divine intelligence all about me, in the flower, the tree, the brook and the meadow. I know that the intelligence that created all these things is in me and around me and that I can call upon it for my slightest need.

I know that my body is a manifestation of pure spirit and that spirit is perfect; therefore my body is perfect also. I enjoy life, for each day brings a constant demonstration of the power and wonder of the universe and myself. I am confident. I am serene. I am sure. No matter what obstacle or undesirable circumstance crosses my path, I refuse to accept it, for it is nothing but illusion. There can be no obstacle or undesirable circumstance to the mind of God, which is in me, and around me, and serves me now.

CPSIA information can be obtained
at www.ICGtesting.com
Printed in the USA
LVHW020747301020
669991LV00005B/5